M000282003

Advance Praise for *Status Dynamics*

"A fascinating meta-framework for psychotherapy based on original and integrative insights from Descriptive Psychology. This is one of those rare books for therapists at all stages of development, from beginners to masters."

William J. Doherty, Ph.D.,
Professor and Director of the
Marriage and Family Therapy Program
University of Minnesota,
Author of Soul Searching

"Whatever your therapeutic orientation, the status considerations contained in this book should give you an additional and powerful means to intervene and produce benefits with your therapy clients."

Richard Driscoll, Ph.D.,
Author of Pragmatic Psychotherapy *and* The Binds That Tie:
Overcoming Standoffs and Stalemates in Love Relationships

Praise for Dr. Bergner's previous work, *Pathological Self-Criticism: Assessment and Treatment*

"What a delight to read! The writing is absolutely lucid, and as such the ideas are readily understandable to the reader. The clinical base of the book is absolutely superb. It gives us a model of a warm, caring, and effective therapist. Lastly, the scholarly basis of the volume is first rate."

C.R. Snyder,
Graduate Training Program in Clinical Psychology
University of Kansas
Author of The Psychology of Hope: You Can Get There From Here

"Dr. Bergner has written a wonderful book that provides a very balanced yet provocative examination of maladaptive self-criticism. His book represents an essential reference for researchers and scholars interested in understanding the dynamics of self-criticism and for practitioners who are interested in transforming maladaptive self-criticism into more constructive processes with their clients."

Edward C. Chang, Ph.D.,
Associate Editor, Journal of Social and Clinical Psychology
Incoming Associate Editor, Cognitive Therapy and Research
Department of Psychology
University of Michigan

"Bergner has written a comprehensive plan for the assessment and treatment of people where pathological self-criticism is an issue... The conceptual framework outlined by Bergner and illustrated by the many case examples resonates well to clinical exerience. Therapists will recognize the people described in the case examples; the client's statements will have a familiar ring...Therapists will find this book to have considerable appeal...Clinicians in training will find the close tie-ins of therapeutic intervention with theory and literature review most satisfying..."

Contemporary Psychology, 1997, 42, 627-628.

Status Dynamics

Also by Raymond M. Bergner:

Studies in Psychopathology: The Descriptive Psychology Approach
published by Descriptive Psychology Press, 1993.

Pathological Self-Criticism: Assessment and Treatment
published by Plenum, 1995.

Status Dynamics

Creating New Paths to Therapeutic Change

Raymond M. Bergner, Ph.D.

BURNS PARK
PUBLISHERS

ANN ARBOR

Copyright © 2007 by Raymond M. Bergner

Published by Burns Park Publishers
P. O. Box 4239
Ann Arbor, MI 48106
www.burnsparkpublishers.com

All rights reserved. No part of this publication may be reproduced, stored on a retrieval system, or transmitted in any form or by any means, electronic, mechanical, photocopying, filming, recording or otherwise without prior permission in writing from the publisher.

PEANUTS: © United Feature Syndicate, Inc.

ISBN: 978-0-9772286-1-4

Library of Congress Cataloging-in-Publication Data

Bergner, Raymond M.
   Status dynamics : creating new paths to therapeutic change / Raymond M.
   Bergner. -- 1st ed.
       p. cm.
   Includes bibliographical references and index.
   ISBN 978-0-9772286-1-4 (alk. paper)
   1. Counseling psychology. 2. Problem solving. 3. Change (Psychology) I.
   Title.

   BF636.6.B47 2007
   158'.3--dc22

2007022216

Manufactured in the United States of America

First Edition

10   9 8 7 6 5 4 3 2 1

Contents

Acknowledgments

I wish to express my gratitude, first of all, to the late Dr. Peter G. Ossorio. Had Dr. Ossorio not created the extraordinary intellectual edifice that is Descriptive Psychology, and within that edifice a very powerful set of ideas for the understanding and remediation of psychological problems, the present work quite simply would not exist.

I wish further to thank Jim Holmes, who, as my collaborator on a published article from which chapter 4 of this book evolved, contributed many of the ideas in that chapter. My thanks also to Laurie Bergner, Carolyn Zeiger, Tony Putman, Ana Bridges, and Robyn Walter for their very helpful critiques of a previous version of this manuscript; to Susan Messer for providing the thorough editorial review that I believe has made this work far more interesting and enjoyable to read; and to Ralph Wechsler, Wynn Schwartz, Keith Davis, C.J. Peek, Jim Holmes, Amy Flack, Dan Davis, and Richard Heinrich for providing feedback on selected portions of this work.

Finally, my special thanks go to my publisher, Tony Putman of Burns Park Publishers, for his ongoing support and provision of many helpful ideas in the creation and marketing of this book.

Preface

The status dynamic therapist occupies a world of places. Our particular interest is in places that carry power – places from which our clients can act effectively in their worlds to bring about personal change. As active agents of change, our interest is in helping our clients occupy such positions of power. We position them to fight downhill battles, not uphill ones, to be "in the driver's seat" instead of the passenger seat. We help them approach their problems as proactive, in-control actors, not helpless victims. We want them to attack these problems from the position of acceptable, sense-making, care-meriting persons who bring ample strengths, resources, and past successes to the solution of their difficulties. We help them to proceed from reconstructed worlds, and from places within these worlds, in which they are eligible and able to participate in life in meaningful and fulfilling ways.

Everything that will be said in this book, in one way or another, centers around this core agenda. To further it

- We assign certain empowering statuses – places of power – to our clients based, not on observation, but on the fact alone that our clients are fellow persons (chapter 2).
- We assist our clients in reconstructing both their worlds and their places within their worlds (chapter 3).
- We assist our clients in changing their self-concepts, circumventing that concept's notorious resistance to change by utilizing the largely unrecognized truth that "status takes precedence over fact" (chapter 4).
- We co-create with our clients formulations of their problems in which they are the active initiators of certain "linchpin" factors at the heart of their difficulties, and thus are already in positions of power from which to bring about broad changes in their lives (chapter 5).
- We assist our clients in accepting these new conceptions of themselves and their worlds by adhering to certain policy guidelines

such as "appealing to what matters" to them and "going where we are welcome" (chapter 6).
- We communicate places of power for our clients to occupy through the vehicle of stories and other images (chapter 7).
- Finally, in all that we do, we endeavor to be credible persons so that our clients will accept our status assignments.

My colleagues and I have found the ideas put forward in this book extraordinarily helpful and powerful over the course of several decades. I hope that they will prove of equal value to you and your clients.

Raymond M. Bergner
Normal, Illinois
January, 2007

Chapter 1
A Further Path to Therapeutic Change

"This is a book for clinicians, and I mean it to be clinically useful."

--Irvin Yalom (1980, p. 16)

As psychotherapists, our primary time-honored paths to change have been through modifying our clients' behaviors, cognitions, insights into unconscious factors, and patterns of interaction with significant others. This book presents a further powerful therapeutic option – that of bringing about changes in our clients' *statuses*, an approach referred to as *"status dynamics."* To get an initial sense of this approach in clinical practice, consider the following case example.

"The Servant"

Sharon, a 37-year-old special education teacher and mother, entered psychotherapy for severe marital problems. She felt completely exploited and taken for granted by Jim, her second husband, who was a university professor with a successful career as a scientific researcher. Jim regarded her as almost a servant, she said, a second class citizen whose duty was to care for all the day-to-day mundane tasks so that he could freely pursue his research. Sharon's first marriage had ended in divorce, and even though she felt as though she was failing for a second time, she saw no way out of her current marital difficulties short of leaving her husband.

Sharon described her attempts to achieve equal status with Jim over the five years of their marriage. Her primary strategy had been to "try to be a good wife." By this, she meant that she assumed virtually all the child care and other family responsibilities on top of her own full-time job, demanded little of Jim, and tried in many ways to maintain the harmony at home that he considered vital to success in his career. However, she related, Jim merely accepted this as his due, which led her to her second basic tactic: confronting him angrily about his attitude and behavior. The result? A fierce counterattack and prolonged bitter conflict.

Sharon feared that her position was hopeless. She saw herself as thoroughly victimized, and had no idea how she could change her marriage so that she could be a valued, respected, and equal partner to Jim.

It seemed to me that Sharon would benefit greatly if she could occupy a relational position – a *status* – that would give her the power and leverage to bring about meaningful change. As it happened, she already occupied such a position of power, but had never recognized it. To help Sharon realize this position, I used a characteristic status dynamic technique, that of communicating through *images* (see chapter 7). The specific image I created for Sharon and shared with her was the following: "One evening, a woman went to a party sponsored by a club to which she belonged. She arrived, went directly to the refreshment table, picked up a tray of drinks, and walked around all evening serving her fellow members. At the end of the evening, a friend asked how she had enjoyed the party. 'I hated it'! she replied angrily, 'Hardly anyone talked to me. You'd have thought I wasn't even there. I just felt used and taken for granted, like I wasn't even a member of the club'."

By telling this story, I hoped to shift Sharon's perception of her position at home away from one of helpless victim. Instead, I wanted her to see that she was actively adopting a certain stance toward her husband, and that he in turn was responding in understandable and predictable (if not condonable) ways. Sharon understood the metaphor, and recognized her servile and deferential pattern of behavior as a longstanding one, not only in her marriage, but in her other relationships. She became aware for the first time that she was in charge of a certain mode of behaving and thus to a considerable degree of its predictable interpersonal consequences.

Once Sharon moved to this level of awareness, I addressed and treated her at all times as a responsible author of her servile behaviors. Thus, I never asked her anything like, "How can you extract yourself from the terrible mistreatment you are subject to?" Instead, I repeatedly and in various ways posed the following basic question: "Do you want to put down that tray, or would you prefer to hold onto it?" For example, in one session, I expressed to Sharon that she was "sending out a servant to do a woman's work." With this expression, I meant to communicate that she was both a proactive initiator and a person of authority, and as such distinct from the servant role she was enacting. In other words, it was not her "nature" or her "lot in life" to be servile towards others, either of which would have left her a victim.

By way of further example, as a homework assignment early in therapy, I directed Sharon to play the servant role consciously, deliberately, and even exaggeratedly during the following week, and to notice any advantages or pleasures she realized in doing so. My main reason for doing this was to enhance her sense of ownership and control over her servile actions, as well as her awareness of their possible advantages. She accepted the assignment and reported back the following week that she had carried it out diligently, albeit with considerable self-consciousness and difficulty. In response to this, we explored a question that only a person in a position of responsible authorship could entertain: "Are you willing to give up these pleasures and advantages ?"

Progress with Sharon, who had adopted this deferential stance in life for many years, was slow but substantial over a course of 28 therapeutic sessions. At termination, and again at a six month follow-up, she reported a drastic shift from her servile mode of relating to others (including her husband) to a far more egalitarian one, and stated that she found this very satisfying. In addition, she reported that her husband now showed her much more respect, and now seemed to notice and appreciate the efforts she made to care for their home and family, even though these were more modest than they had been previously. While her marriage remained less than ideal, she experienced considerable satisfaction with it, and was no longer tempted to pursue divorce.

Status Dynamics: The Key Idea

The clinical framework used in Sharon's case, that of *status dynamics*, is concerned with clients' *statuses* as crucial determinants of their behavior. The term "status," as employed here, means essentially *relational position* or *place*. All individuals occupy a variety of positions in relation to everything in their world, and these are their statuses. In Sharon's case, the particular status we focussed on was that of low-power victim. In psychotherapy, the kinds of statuses that frequently come into play include the following:

1. A client's position in relation to the presenting concern. Examples of this would include low-power victim or in-control perpetrator.
2. A client's position in relation to himself or herself. Examples here might include hater, blamer, or harsh critic of oneself.
3. A client's positions in relation to significant others – for example, scapegoat in one's family of origin, pursuer of a distancing spouse, or victim of harassment in one's workplace.
4. A client's stigmatized positions in society – for example, "crazy," "gay," or member of an "undesirable" religious, ethnic, or racial group.
5. Clients' positions that have been crystallized in self-imposed and/or other-imposed labels such as "loser," "mental case," "dummy," or "bad seed."

From a clinical perspective, the crucial point of focussing on clients' statuses is that the occupation of certain relational positions restricts their eligibilities, opportunities, and reasons to act – that is, their "behavior potential" – while the occupation of others expands this potential. To see what I mean, consider for a moment a non-clinical analogy: the military system and its rank structure. In this system, an individual might be a "private" or a "general." Status dyamics would underscore the basic fact that the *mere occupation* of the position of general by an individual carries with it a greatly expanded power and range of possible behaviors than that of private. For example, a general, unlike a private, can give orders to virtually everyone else in the chain of command, can enjoy a host of officers' privileges, and can have a far greater voice in important decisions. Furthermore, this greater behavior potential is completely independent of all the factors historically stressed by clinical theories: the general's beliefs, behavioral skills, motives, biochemical states, or other personal characteristics. Status dynamics emphasizes the fact that *all relational positions carry with them varying degrees of behavior potential.* When Sharon is able simply to move from her initial position of perceived victim to that of proactive, in-control, initiater of her behavior, this shift carries with it a tremendous increase in her power to overcome her problem.

In status dynamic psychotherapy, therapists use these facts about statuses and the behavior potential inherent in them to benefit their clients. The primary goal is to bring about positive change through *status enhancement.* By this I mean that we can assist our clients by literally *assigning* them positions of enhanced power and eligibility, and by consistently *treating* them as occupants of these positions. Should they accept these new positions, they may then act from them to overcome their present limitations and achieve desired life goals.

As is so often the case, what is simple in the saying can be complex and difficult in the doing. It is the same here. For the present, however, I shall leave these complexities to ensuing chapters, and turn my attention to a few remaining introductory matters.

Historical Applications of the Status Dynamic Approach

Status dynamic thinking is not a recent invention. In publications since the 1970s, it has been applied to a wide array of human problems: schizophrenia, depression, manic states, paranoia, suicide, obsessive-compulsive personality, histrionic personality, bulimia, paraphilias and other sexual addictions, incest survivor syndrome, pathogenic self-criticism, meaninglessness, impulsive behavior, alcoholic relationships, maladaptive emotional states, and problems of adolescence. Further, as the case of Sharon illustrates, status dynamic interventions are useful for the many clients who do not suffer from any Axis I DSM disorder, but are struggling with other debilitating problems in living. Finally, a number of broadly usable status dynamic interventions – ones employable for a wide variety of different disorders and problems in living – have been described in previous publications. The interested reader will find sources pertaining to all of these topics in the reference section of this book.

Status Dynamics Coordinates with Other Approaches

Another important point for therapists: status dynamic ideas and interventions may be used alone, but more frequently are used in conjunction with other time-honored techniques such as cognitive restructuring, behavior rehearsal, the conveyance of important insights, or the alteration of familial transactional patterns. To return to Sharon's story, one can easily see how in the course of her therapy, I could have guided her in rehearsing new assertive behaviors, modifying maladaptive beliefs about her entitlements in relation to other people, or assigning homework that called for a departure from the structural patterns currently existing in her marriage. In my own clinical experience, employing status dynamic ideas has proven not only compatible with these other kinds of interventions, but has enhanced the efficacy of all of them.

Outline of this Book

What can you expect from the rest of this book? Aside from further exploration of the central concepts I have presented here, you will find many applications of these ideas to the practice of psychotherapy. These will be organized in the following way.

What can you expect from the rest of this book? Aside from further exploration of the central concepts I have presented here, you will find many applications of these ideas to the practice of psychotherapy. These will be organized in the following way.

Chapter 2: Creating a positive therapeutic relationship. This chapter presents a unique and powerful approach to the positive therapeutic relationship – one in which we as therapists assign certain predetermined statuses to our clients and treat them consistently as holders of these statuses. This approach incorporates the invaluable in-sights of Carl Rogers, but goes beyond them to provide a richer, more elaborated, and more impactful conception of the positive therapeutic relationship.

Chapter 3: Status dynamics, worlds, and world reconstruction. Words have the power to transform worlds. A mother says to her 16 year old son, "Johnny, the man you have always thought was your father is not really your father." One's beloved unexpectedly declares, "I love you; will you marry me?" With such words, an individual's whole world could be radically transformed. But what exactly *is* a "world?" How do worlds work? And how can we as therapists harness the power of words to transform persons' whole worlds for the better? Going beyond, but in no way diminishing the established value and efficacy of cognitive approaches such as those pioneered by Aaron Beck and Albert Ellis, chapter 3 presents status dynamic ideas for tranforming clients' entire worlds.

Chapter 4: A status dynamic approach to changing clients' self-concepts. As psychotherapists, we have long regarded an individual's self-concept as an important determinant of his or her ability to function well. However, we have lacked an adequate, therapeutically useful account of the self-concept. For example, the common view that the self-concept is an organized informational summary of perceived facts about oneself fails to explain why self-concepts tend not to change in the face of seemingly disconfirming facts, even when those facts are positive and the individual acknowledges them to be true. The questions of how to understand – and thus how to get around – this resistance to change, have important implications for psychotherapy. Chapter 4 presents a radically different, status dynamic formulation of the self-concept, and discusses its substantial therapeutic applications and advantages.

Chapter 5: Status dynamics and clinical case formulation. Clinical assessment would ideally organize all the key facts of a case around a single "linchpin" factor, integrating all the information obtained and identifying the core state of affairs from which the client's difficulties issue. When we as therapists can detect the presence of such a central organizing factor, we can proceed in an efficient, economical, non-piecemeal fashion. Further, we can do so without paying the price of superficiality, since we are getting to the heart of the matter for our clients. Finally, in a linchpin formulation, we have a blueprint that provides a clear central goal that we and our clients can pursue together, a clarification for our clients of where their power for solving their problems lies, and a potent source of ideas regarding how we might bring about change. Chapter 5 explores the nature of linchpin formulations, their multifold clinical advantages, and guidelines for creating them.

Chapter 6: The use of therapeutic policies. Recently, an important topic in the field of psychotherapy has been the exploration of common factors – factors that transcend and are critical to the success of a wide variety of therapeutic approaches. Chapter 6 presents a set of time-tested *policies*, or *choice principles* for the effective conduct of psychotherapy. These policies may be regarded as common factors. Though generated in connection with status dynamic psychotherapy, therapists can follow them profitably in connection with any therapeutic approach.

Chapter 7: Using therapeutic images. This chapter falls within an old tradition in psychotherapy, that of story-telling. The chapter describes the therapeutic use of *"images"*, using stories, metaphors, or analogies to capture the essence of clients' dilemmas in helpful ways. A distinguishing characteristic of the status dynamic approach to images is that we as therapists can use them as *diagnoses*, that is, as descriptions that capture the precise nature of what is going wrong. Such diagnoses have many advantages for our clients such as cognitive organization, easy intelligibility, enhanced precision, freedom from stigmatizing implications, and the illumination of paths to change. Chapter 7 relates the many benefits that employing images can have, provides guidelines for presenting, clarifying, and applying them to clients' unique situations, and introduces a number of broadly useful therapeutic images that can be employed with a variety of clients.

****

As a longtime psychotherapist, I am a believer in the power and efficacy of many of the great schools of therapy: cognitive-behavioral, family systems, person-centered, solution-focussed, and psychoanalytic, to mention but a few. I use ideas from all of these schools in my own therapy. Status dynamic interventions are not meant to *replace* the invaluable contributions of these schools, but to *supplement* them. In effect, in writing this book I am saying: "Here is something new and powerful to *add* to your therapeutic understandings and procedures." I believe that you – and your clients – will benefit greatly from these ideas.

Chapter 2
The Therapuetic Relationship

*"Treat a man as he is and he will remain as he is.
Treat a man as he can and should be, and he will
become as he can and should be."*
--Goethe

The plot of the 1938 film classic, "Boys' Town," can be helpful in understanding the positive therapeutic relationship as conceived in a status dynamic way. In this loosely biographical film, a priest, Father Flanagan, runs a community charged with the care of boys who have been in trouble with the law. His core philosophy is expressed in the motto, "There's no such thing as a bad boy." Consistent with this philosophy, Father Flanagan *pre-conceives* each new boy who enters Boys' Town to be at heart a good boy. In other words, he does so, not on the basis of observation, but *a priori*. Furthermore, there is almost nothing the boy can do to change the priest's view of him. Should the boy misbehave in some manner, this is always seen by Father Flanagan, in one way or another, as a bad or misguided act *by a good boy*. It is never taken as grounds to reconsider the young man's basic status as a good person.

Father Flanagan's philosophy infuses all of his actions toward his boys. Not only does he view them as good, but he unfailingly *treats* them as such. Because the boys regard him as a highly estimable and credible person, his unwavering treatment of them as good eventually leads them to view themselves as he views them. In their own eyes, they become basically good people. Finally, with this recasting of themselves as acceptable individuals, they rethink their basic eligibilities in society. From outcast positions – "delinquents," "bad seeds," "losers," and the like – they see themselves as having moved to positions of full membership in society, and with this as having acquired the enhanced eligibilities for relationsips, vocations, and ways of life that go with this new position.

This story illustrates an informal version of what Ossorio (1978/2005) has termed an "accreditation ceremony." In such ceremonies, one person, who occupies a position of high status and credibility, regards other individuals in a highly affirming and accrediting way, and steadfastly treats them accordingly. This accrediting treatment benefits these individuals when they accept the statuses assigned, resulting in significantly enhanced conceptions of themselves and their eligibilities to participate in society.

Conceived as an ongoing, informal version of such an accreditation ceremony, the positive *therapeutic relationship* comprises the following elements:

1. The therapist assigns certain accrediting statuses to the client on an a priori basis.
2. The therapist treats the client accordingly.
3. The client regards the therapist as a credible status assigner.
4. The client recognizes the status assignments that the therapist is making.
5. The client accepts the therapist's status assignments, that is, appraises himself or herself in these ways.

Let's examine each of these elements in turn.

Element #1: Therapist Assigns Accrediting Statuses

Consider the following events that occurred at the outset of one woman's therapy. Andrea, a young, married, mother of a 5 year old son, came to therapy visibly shaken by an incident that had occurred two days previously. Asked by her therapist, Robyn, what had happened, Andrea responded that she had begun to take her son out for a visit to the park. The temperature outside was in the 50's and so it did not occur to her to put a hat on him. As she and her son were leaving the house, her husband, who was watching a football game, looked over and remarked, "Aren't you going to put a hat on that kid?" In response to this, Andrea exploded in anger. Her husband in turn lashed out at her: "What the hell is wrong with you? I ask you a simple question and you blow up. What is the deal here? A simple question and you drop the atom bomb. You're just losing it. I think you should go see a shrink." This comeback shook Andrea profoundly. It caused her to believe that her husband might be right, that her response was completely out of proportion to what he had said, was therefore highly irrational, and thus meant that she had some sort of mental illness.

Hearing Andrea's story, Robyn's conviction, every bit as ingrained as Father Flanagan's about his boys' goodness, was that Andrea did make sense, and that she was to be treated accordingly in their therapeutic relationship. Robyn believed, indeed assumed a priori, that Andrea's every behavior and emotional reaction, including the present one, had an inherent logic and represented an understandable way of looking at things. Proceeding on this basis, Robyn asked Andrea a series of simple questions, which are condensed and paraphrased here.

Robyn: "Your husband's remark related to your ability to make good judgments as a mother – basically, to your competence as a mother. How important an area of your life is this?"

Andrea: "Extremely important."

Robyn: "So, in saying what he said, he is criticizing you about a very important and sensitive matter."

Andrea: "Yes."

Robyn: "Now, is this an isolated incident, or has this happened before?"

Andrea: "No, he does it all the time. He's always second guessing, always criticizing what I do as a mother."

Robyn: "Hmm, so, thinking about this here today, in saying what he said Saturday, did this seem to you at all like a last straw, like it had happened over and over and you just couldn't stand it one more time?"

Andrea: "Yes, that seems right now that you say it."

Robyn: "So I'm beginning to see why you would be so angry. Being a good mother is terribly important to you. You make what seems a very reasonable decision to take your son to the park without a hat. But your husband criticizes the decision you made as a mother. And it's not an isolated incident. This has happened many times. So, it's the last straw for you and you understandably react in a very strong way."

Andrea (visibly relieved): "Yes, that's all true. I guess my reaction did make sense."

With this simple, brief interchange, all initiated by Robyn's a priori belief that Andrea made sense and her determination to regard and treat her as such, Robyn was able to relieve Andrea's profound concern that her emotions made no sense and thus that she was having a mental breakdown. Therapy was then able to proceed to a far calmer exploration of how the issues between Andrea and her husband might best be approached and resolved.

As noted in chapter one, the term "status" means relational position, and it was stated there that, among other things, this included clients' positions that have become crystallized in self-imposed and/or other-imposed labels such as "mental case," "loser," "dummy," or "bad seed." Further it was stated that each of a person's various statuses corresponds to some "behavior potential." That is, to be in any relational position is to have greater or lesser eligibility and/or opportunity to engage in certain behaviors.

Sociological statuses such as "military general," "boss" or "father" are clear examples of statuses that carry with them behavior potential. Less clear is the fact that personal attribute labels, which are usually understood as referring to attributes inhering "in" persons, also designate such statuses. Charles Schulz, however, in a Charlie Brown cartoon many years ago, appreciated this fact very well. In this cartoon, we find Charlie Brown lamenting that, because he is a "Nothing" and a much-desired little red-haired girl is a "Something," he can't go over and have lunch with her. Charlie understands that his self-assigned label, "Nothing," is not merely the name of some attribute of his, but is also a *status*. This label *places* or *locates* him somewhere in the scheme of things. In this instance, it is a place of tremendous ineligibility to relate to others whom he deems worthy, and in the episode we see that Charlie is in fact unable to approach the little girl. To contradict an old children's saying, names *can* really hurt you.

In the same way, other personal characteristic concepts such as "mentally disturbed," "irrational," "honest," or "trustworthy" refer both to attributes and to statuses. When we appraise Joe as an honest person, we are not merely seeing him as having a certain attribute. We are also assigning him to a place or position in our worlds such that we are prepared to treat him quite differently from Jack, whom we take to be dishonest. When Andrea appraises herself as "mentally disturbed," she assigns herself a position that is quite different than "sane" or "rational," and she treats herself and her actions quite differently. For example, regarding herself as sane and rational, she would trust her judgments far more, and act upon them with far greater confidence than if she believes herself crazy or irrational.

Statuses can be assigned a priori. Most often, we assign statuses to others on the basis of observation. We observe Joe, and see that he has the statuses "lieutenant," "father," "honest person," "Jack's rival," "his own harshest critic," and so forth.

However, it is possible to make status assignments that are not based on observation – that are made *a priori*. We have already seen this in the case of Father Flanagan and his view of the boys at Boys' Town, and in the case of Robyn and her view of Andrea. A familiar example of a priori status assignment from everyday life occurs in jury trials, where jurors are instructed, prior to any observation, to regard defendants as "innocent until proven guilty." Another, more clinically relevant example occurs frequently in the context of positive therapeutic relationships. Following the pioneering example of Carl Rogers, many psychotherapists assign the status "unconditionally acceptable" to new clients from the moment they enter the consultation room. Their position is not the openly empirical, "Well, let's wait and see if this person seems like an acceptable individual." It is instead the a priori, "As a human being, this person is unconditionally acceptable; I will regard him or her as such to the degree that I am able."

Accrediting and degrading status assignments can be made. A status assignment is *accrediting* when its acceptance entails the acceptance of expanded eligibilities and/or opportunities to participate in a community. For example, should Lucy, in one of her five cent psychiatric sessions, characterize Charlie Brown as a "Something," and he accept this characterization, he would then appraise himself as eligible for relationships with others whom he sees as worthwhile "Somethings." Likewise, if a therapy client, through experiencing a therapeutic relationship in which she was accepted unconditionally, came to regard herself as acceptable, her new self-appraisal would carry with it a perception of herself as eligible for acceptance from others.

A status assignment is *degrading* when its acceptance entails the acceptance of diminished eligibilities and/or opportunities for participation in a community. This would occur, for example, if one person branded another a "nothing," a "loser," or, as in Andrea's case, a "mentally disturbed person," and the second person accepted this label as valid.

In a positive therapeutic relationship, then, the therapist makes a priori status assignments to the client that are accrediting in nature, and treats him or her accordingly. Where Carl Rogers focussed on the single status "unconditionally acceptable," however, the status dynamic therapist builds his or her therapeutic relationship around nine different statuses. These are the following:

1. One Who Is Acceptable

As Rogers emphasized in his work, countless clients believe themselves unacceptable persons. They neither accept themselves nor regard themselves as worthy of the acceptance of other persons. A therapeutic relationship in which the client is assigned the status "acceptable," – meaning one in which he or she is *in fact accepted* by the therapist – can therefore be highly beneficial for these clients. Further, such a relationship enhances the likelihood that our other interventions will be effective, since clients are more likely to listen to and cooperate with therapists who accept them than ones who do not.

2. One Who Makes Sense

It is enormously self-disqualifying to see oneself as making no sense. Many clients, based on the attributions of others, or through their own second-guessing, doubt-casting, or outright dismissive reactions to themselves and their decisions, have come to believe that their perceptions, emotions, judgments and decisions are inadequately grounded in reality and/or that they are without logical foundation. When individuals continually undermine themselves in such ways, they increasingly regard themselves as unqualified to make competent judgments and take appropriate action. The degree to which such a belief about oneself undermines all of one's judgments and behavior can be staggering in certain cases.

In the therapeutic relationship, therefore, we as therapists, like Robyn with Andrea, would do well to view our clients a priori as *ineligible to make no sense*. In practice, this means that the client's every emotion, judgment, and action has an inherent logic, and that his or her every perception is an understandable way of looking at things. Clients might be *mistaken* in their perceptions, judgments, and views, but they do make sense.

Before leaving this topic, a few brief comments are in order regarding its application to psychotic individuals. First, the policy cannot be applied in those cases where our clients' symptoms are primarily biological in origin. Second, aside from such cases, there is a substantial literature attesting to the social intelligibility of psychotic behavior that is quite helpful in enabling us to understand its underlying sense. When we are able to be sensitive to the meanings and strategic implications of so-called "crazy" behavior, we are able to respond to such behavior with more understanding, and thus more competently. For example, one psychotic young man, in response to his therapist's wish that he "have a nice Christmas," responded to her by saying "Francis Gary Powers." The therapist, fortunately blessed with a knowledge of history and a gift for word puzzles, recognized this as a veiled positive wish. (Knowing that Francis Gary Powers was the American pilot implicated in the famous 1960 U-2 spy plane incident, she understood that he was saying "you too!"). Although most of us could be forgiven for not being able to grasp such a riddle on the spot, this therapist was able to respond more sensitively and appropriately than another therapist who might dismiss the young man's rejoinder as nonsensical "word salad."

3. One Whose Best Interests Come First

Generally, individuals who assign themselves the status "unlovable" are persons who believe that their welfare and best interests could not be of genuine concern to others. If the actions of others towards them seem positive, it cannot be because those others truly care about them and their best interests, and they will tend to generate alternative explanations of such actions (e.g., the other person "must want something.") In contrast, people who believe they are lovable see themselves as eligible and worthy to have others truly care about them and their personal welfare.

Clearly, then, clients benefit when we as therapists assign them the status of "one whose best interests come first in this relationship." In practice, this means that our fundamental commitment is to conduct therapy first and foremost for the benefit of the client, not the benefit of society, the client's family, the therapist, or any other party. Such a therapeutic stance is an accreditation in which the status assignment has to do with lovability. That is, it has to do with that aspect of love which is essential to all forms of that relationship (romantic, parental, altruistic, etc.): a genuine investment in the wellbeing of another person for that person's own sake.

4. One Who Is an Agent

Many clients view themselves as helpless pawns of internal or external forces. They convey this in expressions like "something came over me," "I found myself doing such and such," "so-and-so made me do it," and the like. They convey this, further, when they portray themselves as helpless in the face of their "impulses," their longstanding habits, their personal histories, or their "natures." A "pawn of forces" (e.g., a puppet or a robot) is incapable of self-determination – of considering behavioral options and choosing from among them. A pawn is powerless.

In contrast, to be an agent is to be capable of entertaining behavioral options and choosing from among them. To be an agent is to have control, albeit imperfect, of one's behavior. To be an agent is to have power. Thus, personal agency is included here as a vital component of a positive therapeutic relationship. We treat people as persons, and not as exemplars of some species of biologically, environmentally, or otherwise determined organic machine.

5. One Who Is Significant

To be insignificant is to be, like Charlie Brown, a "Nothing" living in a world of "Somethings," and to suffer the relational ineligibilities that go with this. It is to be an unimportant "nobody," a cipher, in a world peopled by important "somebodies." It is to live in an "I don't count-you count" world. When we as therapists can assign to a client a place of genuine importance and significance in our lives, then, this is a vital accreditation. In practice, we express this in behaviors such as listening very carefully and respectfully to clients, bestowing our undivided attention on them during the therapy hour, remembering the content of previous sessions, initiating therapeutic actions beyond the session if needed (e.g., writing strategic letters), and striving in any other way to convey to the client that "you are not just another 'case' among many that I am paid to direct my attention to for fifty minutes each week."

6. One Who Is To Be Given the Benefit of the Doubt

Within bounds of realism, we as therapists have options regarding how we construe our clients. These options often differ in the degree to which they embody an accrediting or degrading understanding of something. For example, a mother, Sylvia, is overly concerned about her child's safety. As therapists, we might view her either (a) as someone who harbors an unconscious hatred of her child, or (b) as someone who is utterly convinced that, for one such as her, nothing so good as her child and their relationship can possibly be lasting. The relational recommendation here is to treat the client as one who is to be given the benefit of the doubt. Given a choice among different ways of looking at a client, choose as a matter of policy the most status-enhancing, yet realistic, possibility.

7. One Who Has Strengths and Resources

An individual who possessed no strengths or resources – no enabling abilities, traits, ideas, motives, or positions of power – would be a completely helpless individual. Such a person would not have the ability to act to improve his or her own life. The therapist who undertook therapy with the implicit assumption that, "This client is a completely helpless person, and I shall have to proceed from there," would be starting from an almost impossible position.

As therapists, then, we are well-advised to assume a priori that each of our clients possesses strengths and resources – that he or she possesses enabling abilities, traits, knowledge, motives, roles, and/or positions of leverage. In this approach, the therapeutic task becomes one of *finding, recognizing, and utilizing* strengths and resources, not of determining whether or not they exist. This perspective, known as the principle of "utilization," is a mainstay of Ericksonian and solution-focussed approaches to psychotherapy.

8. One Who Is the Therapist's Ally and Collaborator

Being a member of a two-person community in which both persons are pulling together and collaborating to accomplish a common goal is usually status enhancing in two ways. First, if the client views the therapist as an estimable person, the very fact of being related to such a person as an ally and collaborator is itself status enhancing. Second, as the old aphorism that "two heads are better than one" asserts, working in collaborative alliance with another person, particularly one who is expert in the relevant domain, is usually more enabling than working alone. Thus, treating the client as an ally and collaborator is recommended as a key element of a positive therapeutic relationship.

"A priori status assignment" has a somewhat different meaning here than it does elsewhere in this chapter. Where alliance is concerned, we cannot assume at the outset that the client is an ally, in the same sense that we can assume that he or she is acceptable or sense-making. What we can do, however, is to initiate behaviors toward our clients that we would initiate with an ally, thus inviting and encouraging the client to respond in kind (compare: we make the opening move in a board game, thus inviting another to play with us). The client could respond by immediately enacting the complementary role, thus establishing an alliance. Or the client might not do so, thus necessitating additional efforts on our part to establish the alliance.

9. One Who Is a Fellow Status Assigner

From all that has been said thus far in this chapter, you might conclude that, when working in a status dynamic mode, the therapist "hands down" statuses to the client from "on high." In other words, like the Wizard of Oz, he or she hands them down from a position that is superior to that of the client. But this is not at all the spirit of this approach. In fact, to enact these status assignments in that spirit would be degrading to clients.

An important way to avoid such an enactment of the therapeutic relationship is simply to regard our clients as fellow status assigners who are themselves fully eligible to assign statuses to us. In practice, this means that we listen carefully, and above all *give due consideration* to the views of us expressed by our clients, and not permit ourselves to become overly insulated from them. In the end, we might agree or disagree, but the critical elements here are that we genuinely consider them, and that the client recognize that we have done so. A failure to do so occurs, for example, when therapists misuse the notion of "transference" in such a way that they routinely dismiss their clients' reactions to them as "transference distortions."

A Final Comment

In suggesting that all of these status assignments be implemented, I do not mean to imply that all clients come to therapy feeling degraded in all of these ways. Clearly, they do not. However, even in those cases where they do not feel so degraded, to eliminate any one of these status assignments from the therapeutic relationship would be a serious mistake. For example, even if a client already believed herself to be a rational, sense-making person, we would obviously be remiss if we regarded and treated her as not making sense, since in doing so we might undermine her sense of her own rationality. The elimination of any of the relational elements listed above creates the danger of a countertherapeutic, degrading relationship between therapist and client in which important statuses that the client possessed initially might be undermined by the therapist's degrading treatment.

Element #2: Therapist Treats The Client Accordingly

A terminally ill patient is verbally reassured that she is not going to die, but is *treated* as a dying person. A child is told that he is coordinated, but treated as clumsy. A client is told that he is rational, but is treated as someone who is always misreading reality. In cases such as these, actions generally speak louder than words. In therapy, this means that the status assignments implicit in the way we as therapists *treat* clients "speak louder" than those contained in our verbal messages, and it is these status assignments that are more likely to be "heard" by our clients. In cases where our verbalized status assignments are congruent with the way we treat the client, it is the treatment that authenticates the words, and not the other way around.

The lesson? As therapists, we must not only make accrediting a priori status assignments; we must also persistently treat clients in a manner that is consistent with those status assignments. Our relational task is *to see to it that the client is successful in our relationship in the precise ways delineated by the status names.* In other words, our task is to see to it, to the extent that we are able, that in this relationship the client *is* acceptable, *does* make sense, *is* significant, and so forth. When conditions are optimal, this process tends to occur smoothly, naturally, and automatically. We simply see our clients as acceptable, as making sense, as "Somethings," and so forth, and naturally treat them accordingly.

When conditions are less than optimal, however, treating the client in accrediting ways may require considerable ingenuity and work. For example, a client might report that he has been sent by the courts for sexually abusing his child and, despite his facade of earnestness, we can see that his attitude is quite cavalier and that he has come to therapy primarily to avoid court sanctions. Our first reaction to him is nonaccepting, and this attitude will often be expressed in our behavior, even when we try to appear accepting. In such a case, we must try to do something that permits us to genuinely regard and treat this client in an accrediting manner. We might, for example, actively search for a new perspective on this man by asking extensively about his history, current circumstances, and reasons for being sexually involved with his child. The key requirement for acceptance will be that we get an understanding of this man that enables us to accept him, but without condoning or excusing his destructive actions. We might learn that he was himself abused, that he is genuinely ignorant of the effects of his actions on his child, that he does care for the child, and/or that he has been drastically degraded as a person in other spheres of his life. Knowledge of any or all of these facts might enable us to accept him better. Of course, searches for more charitable perspectives, examinations of our own countertherapeutic reactions, and other measures designed to put ourselves in a more genuinely accrediting posture will sometimes fail, and we will not be able to accredit certain clients.

Element #3: Client Must See the Therapist As a Valid Status Assigner

Psychotherapy begins with the meeting between therapist and client. If all goes well, the result of this meeting will be the formation of a two-person community, a little community or "world" set apart from the larger community and world. In the status dynamic view, the central purpose of this two-person community is to provide a place where the therapist can enhance the client's status in such a way that the client can participate more fully and rewardingly in the larger community. In order to achieve this goal, it may at times be necessary for this two-person community to possess an extraordinary capability – namely, that it be able to function as the preeminent status-assigning community in the client's world. When this is the case, the therapeutic community acquires the power to preempt and/or to disqualify other persons or groups who are degrading the client illegitimately, such as the family of origin, the spouse, the peer group, or even the broader culture.

If the therapeutic community is to have this power, the therapist must have the kind of standing in the client's eyes that is necessary to function as an effective status assigner. To return to our earlier example, it was only by virtue of his high standing in the eyes of his boys that Father Flanagan could assign to them the status "good boy," and have them accept this status for themselves. Thus, therapists must conduct themselves in ways that are likely to result in the achievement of such standing. In particular, they should seek to establish the following five statuses in the eyes of their clients:

1. One Who is Credible

Clients will not accept our status assignments unless they find us *credible*. In practice, this means that we must strive to be honest, knowledgeable, and competent, and that the client must see us in these ways. Behaviors such as interviewing skillfully, conveying an accurate and empathic understanding of the client, providing explanations that are cogent and compelling, citing relevant research and other literature, presenting ourselves in unobtrusive ways as experienced and successful, dressing and behaving professionally, and creating a physical environment with elements such as books and diplomas that suggest competence are all helpful in achieving credibility with most clients. Behaviors such as denigrating ourselves, conveying undue confusion or tentativeness, espousing theories that appear strange or unconvincing to the client, lying, or behaving unprofessionally will as a rule detract from credibility, and therefore damage our ability to function as a potent status assigners.

2. One Who is His or Her "Own Person"

Clients need to see their therapists as their own persons. That is, they need to see us as persons who are able and willing to state our true positions on issues that arise, to agree or disagree, to cooperate or confront, and to set self-respecting limits on what we will and will not do in relation to them. If the client perceives us as someone who, for example, *has* to be perpetually nice and agreeable, or who holds back our true opinions, they might not perceive us as valid affirmers of their status.

3. One Who is Eligible to Criticize the Culture

Many of our clients have accepted societally based status assignments that are both degrading and debilitating. For example, society might have communicated to them that they must be married, heterosexual, white, thin, highly achieving, sexually unvictimized, and more, or else they may not consider themselves worthwhile. Thus, in the status dynamic view, it is important that we as therapists position ourselves to undermine these inhumane, unjust, and often impossible cultural standards.

One good means for doing this is by ourselves espousing the highest and most enduring values of the culture. A lesson can be learned here from Edward Albee, the playwright, who is an effective critic of America largely because he criticizes it in terms of its own original core values. When we appeal in our sessions to values such as justice, integrity, authenticity, fairness, and responsibility, we present ourselves as subscribers to the highest values of our culture. In doing so, we can function as especially effective critics of this culture in its unreasonable status assigning practices.

4. One Who Knows the Client

Clients can dismiss therapists' accreditations if they doubt that their therapist really knows them. "If my therapist really knew me," they might think, "and if she knew certain things about me, she wouldn't find me so acceptable." Thus therapists must truly know their clients, and clients must know that they are known, or these clients will not be able to assign their therapists the status of "one who really knows and understands me." This point was made long ago by Carl Rogers.

5. One Who Embodies the Statuses Being Assigned

To accredit clients effectively, therapists must themselves be seen as having the same statuses they are assigning. Thus, it is important that clients see their therapists as acceptable, rational, significant, care-meriting people. If our clients see us as, for example, unacceptable or irrational or insignificant, these perceptions will detract from our ability to be effective status assigners. For example, Elizabeth might see her therapist, Todd, as irrational because he seems to make judgments, not on the basis of what seems to her to be realistic and logical, but on the basis of theories that appear implausible to her. In particular, he continually pushes a theory that every woman who has periodic bouts of depression must have been abused as a child, even though Elizabeth finds this implausible and has no recollection of any such abuse. In such a circumstance, Elizabeth's view of Todd as irrational will detract greatly from his ability to function as a credible, potent status assigner.

Recovering from Client Disqualifications

Despite our best efforts, clients will at times disqualify us as legitimate status assigners. They will devalue us as unacceptable, or irrational, or noncredible, or deficient in some other way. When this occurs, it is critically important that we recognize what has happened and take measures to try to restore our lost status. Otherwise, both we and our clients lose.

For example, some clients will devalue and disqualify us precisely because we accept them. The typical logic of this devaluation is captured in the famous quip that "I would never consider joining any club that would have the likes of me for a member." With clients who disqualify us on such grounds, one avenue to recovery of our lost status is simply to share this quip with clients, and use it to give them the necessary insight to question and undo their disqualification.

Element #4: Client Must Recognize The Status Assignment Being Made

Clients need not be fully aware of the therapist's status assignments, nor do they need to be able to articulate them. Still, if they remain totally unaware of them, they cannot possibly accept them, nor can they benefit from the accreditation and enhanced behavior potential that follow from them. As therapists, then, we must pay attention to whether such recognition is occurring. The best policy here is to assume that clients do recognize how they are being treated, unless there are indications to the contrary. Rather than look for every little positive indication, we undertake a far more manageable task: we watch for indications that our status assignments are not registering, and then take appropriate action.

For example, Ana has had 15 therapy sessions with her client, Bill. Although she genuinely likes and accepts him, she is getting clear indications that he sees her accepting actions as merely role behavior, as just "acting like therapists are supposed to act," and nothing more. Ana must do something to change his perceptions. She might, for example, address the matter directly: "Bill, I'm getting the sense that you find it hard to believe that I might actually accept you. You look at my behavior and you think, 'Well, she's acting in an accepting way because that's the way therapists are supposed to act. It couldn't possibly mean that she actually accepts me.' Now, there is no way to prove anything here, and I'm not going to try. But I'd like to suggest that you watch for something. As you feel increasingly better about yourself, I'd like you to notice whether more and more you also come to trust my acceptance of you." Here, Ana is working to raise Bill's consciousness of how he is interpreting events, and to get him to question and rethink his conclusions. In effect, she is posing her acceptance as a fact, but one that Bill's lack of self-acceptance is currently getting in the way of his recognizing.

Element #5: Client Must Accept Accrediting Status Assignments

An accreditation is not complete until the client accepts the status assignment. Just as an employee might refuse a job promotion, an actor turn down an Academy Award, or a person decline a proposal of marriage, a client might reject a therapist's accreditation. The accreditation is then incomplete, and as yet unsuccessful.

- In such circumstances, we as therapists must try to determine why our status assignments have not been accepted, and do what we can to have them accepted. Some possibilities:
- Has the client simply assimilated all that has gone on to her degraded conceptions of herself; for example, continuing to think of herself as a "reject," has she concluded that "It's

amazing how even a reject like me can be accepted by some people.'"?

- Has the client rejected the new statuses because they seem too threatening; for example, sensed that "If I took it that I was really in control of my behavior, was rational, and had strengths, people would expect a lot more of me and hold me accountable – that is a frightening prospect."?

- Have we as therapists failed to unearth some important basis for the client's devalued status, leaving the client thinking "If my therapist knew about X (my affair, abortion, philandering, child abuse, etc.), he wouldn't be so accepting."?

- Has the client sensed that acceptance of the therapist's accreditations would create serious dislocations in other key relationships; for example, "If I took it that my best interests did indeed count, and assertively pursued them, would this jeopardize my relationship with my spouse."?

These and numerous other possibilites might be examined and, when they prove accurate, addressed so as to bring accreditation to completion.

Final Considerations

Dealing With the Danger of External Disconfirmation

It is of course vitally important that a client who has accepted accreditation in the therapist's office be able to maintain that accreditation in the larger world. Thus, a key matter to be considered is whether others in the client's world seem to support or to disconfirm our assigned statuses. If they support them, we can simply go on with the other business of therapy. However, if external disconfirmation is evident or seems likely, what can we do to insulate the client from such disconfirmation?

An example: Jill, a young college student, had long thought of herself as unlovable. She based this appraisal primarily on a childhood in which both of her parents scapegoated her, and her very narcissistic mother grossly rejected her. Further, her mother's continued rejection and blaming attacks were perpetuating Jill's conviction of unlovability. Aside from simply accepting Jill and putting her best interests first in the therapeutic relationship, Jill's therapist, Doug, devised measures to insulate her from her mother's degradations. Doug strongly and repeatedly promoted a picture of reality that portrayed Jill as a "placeholder" in her family of origin. That is, the family needed a scapegoat, and Jill, regardless of her actual merits or value, occupied that position; *anyone* who occupied that position, Doug asserted, would be scapegoated. Further, Doug explained over and over in various ways throughout the therapy that Jill's rather disturbed mother was unfortunately unable to love, and that her failure to love Jill was therefore not in any sense a valid indicator of Jill's lovability. In time, through these efforts to insulate Jill from her mother's degradations, she became relatively immune to them. Ultimately, both through the establishment of an accrediting therapeutic relationship and through these efforts to disqualify her mother as a valid critic, Jill was able to appraise herself as lovable and acceptable to others. Furthermore, she was able to act on this by entering into a new relationship with a man, and by initiating a better relationship with her estranged father.

Modifying the Relationship for Specific Clients

In my experience, I have found it beneficial with certain clients to modify, not the *nature* of the nine status assignments listed above, but the *mode of expression* of these status assignments. For example, where we might be warm and forthcoming in expressing our acceptance of many clients, we are ill-advised to do so with other clients, such as many paranoid ones, who would feel vulnerable and frightened if we approached them in this way. We need in such cases to find ways to convey acceptance that would not threaten or provoke any untoward reaction in these individuals. One such way might be the adoption of a more formal, professional stance in which we would convey acceptance largely through the content of our verbal input to the client. Without multiplying examples, the general point here is that the way in which we enact our status assignments must take into account the personal characteristics of the client if we are to be successful accreditors.

Enacting the Therapeutic Relationship is an Intervention.

A traditional issue in the field of psychotherapy concerns the relative importance of the therapeutic relationship, as opposed to therapeutic interventions, in affecting change. Four general positions have been taken on this issue:

1. Some theorists, most notably those with a person-centered orientation, have maintained that the therapeutic relationship is by itself both necessary and sufficient to bring about therapeutic change.
2. Some cognitive-behavioral theorists have held essentially the opposite view – that a positive therapeutic relationship is neither necessary nor sufficient to produce therapeutic change.
3. A position entertained by other cognitive-behavioral theorists is that a positive therapeutic relationship represents a precondition – a sort of necessary, enabling, but itself noncausal medium – for therapeutic change.
4. Most psychoanalysts and certain behavioral theorists have maintained that the enactment of a positive therapeutic relationship is itself a change-producing intervention, but one that in most cases must be supplemented by further interventions to produce change.

The position presented in this book is consistent with this last one: Enactment of an accrediting therapeutic relationship as described above is itself an intervention. It is something that a therapist *does* to bring about therapeutic change. The therapist's relational behavior is instrumental behavior with a therapeutic end. As such, it qualifies as an intervention every bit as much as correcting a misconception or doing exposure therapy. It is simply a subset of the set of all interventions that we enact as therapists.

Though a subset, it is a *necessary* subset. My experience has been that, when an accrediting therapeutic relationship does not develop, positive therapeutic outcomes rarely ensue. Without such a relationship, we not only fail to accredit the client, but we are also less effective with our other interventions. This observation is consistent with much recent research documenting that a positive therapeutic relationship is a common factor critical to the success of therapies of many different schools.

Because my primary focus here has been on therapeutic change, I have discussed the therapeutic relationship only insofar as it is *instrumental* in bringing about therapeutic goals. In so discussing it, my intention is neither to minimize the *ethical values* inherent in such a relationship (e.g., Kant's famous admonition that we ought to treat every person as an end and not as a means) nor to minimize the *intrinsic value* of this relationship as a personal relationship. It is, for those who can appreciate it, an end in itself, and not merely a means to some further end.

Summary

The therapeutic relationship can be powerfully conducted as an ongoing, informal rite of accreditation. In this relationship, the therapist assigns the client certain predetermined statuses of a highly affirming nature, and steadfastly treats the client accordingly. These statuses include: one who is acceptable, who makes sense, who is an agent, whose best interests are a genuine priority, who is significant, who possesses strengths and resources, who is to be given the benefit of the doubt, who is an ally and collaborator, and who is eligible to assign statuses to the therapist.

If clients are to accept these status assignments, they must regard the therapist as eligible to make them. Thus, therapists must be, and must present themselves as being, honest, competent, their own persons, subscribers to the highest of the culture's values, and possessors of the statuses they are themselves assigning. Finally, therapists must attempt to assess and remove any barriers to clients' recognition and ultimate acceptance of their accrediting status assignments, insulate clients from external degraders, and modify their mode of conveying status assignments in light of the personal characteristics of particular clients.

Chapter 3
Reconstructing Worlds

Words can transform worlds. Consider...

* A doctor says to a patient: "You have cancer, and only six months to live."
* An official from the lottery announces to a poor family: "You have won ten million dollars."
* One spouse unexpectedly says to another: "I've been having an affair for the last two years and I want a divorce."
* Charles Darwin says to everybody: "The world as you find it, including human beings, was not created six thousand years ago; it is far older, and you have evolved from lower species."

This list could go on indefinitely. One could cite, for example, the world transforming effects on millions of people of the words of Christ, Buddha, Gandhi, Copernicus, Einstein, Marx, and many others. In these instances, it isn't, to use Hamlet's phrase, just "words, words, words." *These words are about people's worlds,* about the total psychological environments in which they conduct their lives. All of these words, heard for the first time, convey news that an individual's or a whole society's world has just been transformed in a very dramatic and consequential way.

As therapists, we are presented with opportunities, through our spoken interactions with our clients – through our *words* – to reconstruct their worlds for the better. The purpose of this chapter is to discuss the implications of this for the practicing psychotherapist.

Worlds And How They Work

In chapter 2, I related an abbreviated version of a Charlie Brown dilemma about a little red-haired girl. To better understand what I mean by "worlds," consider this expanded version: Charlie is sitting on the playground eating his lunch. Clearly dejected and with head downcast, he says to a friend who is with him, "I really wish I could go across the playground and have lunch with that little red haired girl, but (sigh!) I can't because she's a something and I'm a nothing. (Musing....) Now if I were a nothing and she were a nothing, I could go over there. Or if I were a something and she were a something, I could go over there. Or if I were a something and she were a nothing, I could go over there. But (sigh!) I'm a nothing and she's a something, so I can't go over and have lunch with her" (from Schulz, 1968).

PEANUTS: © United Feature Syndicate, Inc.

In this example, Charlie introduces us to his world. Although strictly speaking it is only a part of his total world, for purposes of clarity and manageability, we shall let it stand proxy for his total world. This world, as he describes it, is peopled by two classes of persons, "Somethings" and "Nothings." Further, these classes have different eligibilities for entering into and maintaining personal relationships: Somethings are eligible to have relationships with both Somethings and Nothings, while Nothings are confined to relationships with Nothings. Finally, Charlie sees himself as having a place, or status, in this world. In his view, he is one of the Nothings, and is thus ineligible for acceptance by any of the Somethings, including most importantly the much desired red haired girl. It is within this world that Charlie acts, or in this case, refrains from acting.

What is a "World"?

A person's world, as the term is intended here, is a totality. It is, as the person understands the matter, everything both actual and possible. It is the state of affairs that includes all other states of affairs – all actual and possible objects, processes, events, and states of affairs. As such, it is the total psychological environment within which each individual conducts his or her life. This concept of world is reminiscent of, though not the same as, Kurt Lewin's notion of "the self within the life space," and Ludwig Binswanger's concept of "world design."

A person's world is not a random accumulation of facts; it is a unity. Thus, for example, a given person might know that a "rook" is a chess piece with a certain traditional shape and a certain set of move and capture eligibilities. Related to this, she knows (a) its place within the larger context of the game of chess, (b) that chess is but one of many games, (c) that games are but one of many human social practices along with conversing, negotiating differences, making love, educating children, creating art, and many, many others, and (d) that these social practices are largely played out within social institutions such as marriage, family, church, workplace, friendship network, and so forth. Proceeding from her understanding of these more global levels of social practice and institution, she could, if need be, draw connections to countless other discrete facts about the world. Finally, to say that this world knowledge is a unity is not to say that it is totally self-consistent and noncontradictory, but only that everything within it is related to everything else.

As this characterization suggests, it would be extraordinarily difficult, if not impossible, to give a complete description of any person's total world. Fortunately, as clinicians (and as persons living our lives in general), we do not need to do so, and our purposes on any given occasion are well served by capturing the relevant, critical parts of a person's world. Thus, Charlie Brown comes to us for therapy. He is depressed, lonely, and behaviorally immobilized with respect to pursuing the love of his life, the little red-haired girl. To understand his problem, we need to understand, not every aspect of his total world, but only the relevant and significant portions such as those articulated in his theory of "Nothings and Somethings" and his related understanding of his own place and eligibilities within his world. Another client, Kate, comes to us, and we see that many of her problems center around an implicit understanding of human relations as contests, of herself as one of the contestants, and a consequent need always to best others and to be number one; we see further that acting in this world causes her many problems in her relationships. Yet another, Chuck, comes to us and informs us in so many words that "It's a jungle out there; it's eat or be eaten; you have to get them before they get you, and I intend to be the predator, not the prey." Again, we see how acting within this world creates significant problems for him.

People always see discrete facts within a world context. Depending on the perceiver's world, he or she will see the election outcome as marking a "great triumph for my party and the ushering in of a better period for the country," "a devastating defeat for my party," "an insignificant event that makes no real difference in my life," and in many other ways. Marsha, a client of mine whose world was one of self-attributed ugliness, badness, and ineligibility for love, could only see the attentions of a young man at her office as the congenial behavior of someone who was "just being a nice guy." For her, these attentions could not conceivably mean what they seemed to everyone around her to mean: that he was romantically interested in her.

Worlds are constructed. Most people are aware of a distinction between *the real world* and *a person's world*. By the former, we generally mean, not our own private psychological environments in which we are the conscious center, but the world that exists independently of us, that includes us as well as everything else there is, and that will survive our death. For many obvious reasons, the real world and a person's world can never be the same.

- No one person could acquire all the facts there are, and so each of us acquires a different set of facts.
- People are sometimes mistaken in their beliefs, thus creating a disjunction between their beliefs and the real world.
- Some people are capable of observing certain facts that other persons cannot – for example, that the piano is out of tune or that tension exists between the two friends.
- People often interpret events differently and in general see the world differently. One sees a certain remark as a joke, another sees it as an insult. One sees golf as a vital and meaningful human activity, another sees it as a sterile activity in which supposedly mature adults become obsessed with putting little white balls into holes in the ground. One sees life itself as a competition for survival of the fittest, another as the realization

of a divine plan for humankind, and yet another as a "tale told by an idiot, full of sound and fury, signifying nothing." Of the raw stuff of experience and thought, we each *make* quite different things, and it is in this sense that each of us *constructs* our realities or our worlds.

You can't construct "just any old world". Despite the fact that we construct our worlds, there are certain limitations on our world constructions. The real world has a certain recalcitrance such that certain of our beliefs about it cannot be acted upon successfully. For example, if I believe that I can fly unaided, or that a famous movie star is in love with me, or that I can use a rock as a calculator, I will prove unable to act on these beliefs successfully. I can neither fly unaided, successfully presume to have the privileges of the movie star's beloved, nor perform arithmetic operations on a rock. Thus, in the words of Ossorio, "You can't construct just any old world and get away with it." (1998, p. 73). That is, while there is no uniquely correct description of reality, and reality is open to numerous correct descriptions, there are *reality constraints*. Those who are unable to heed these constraints are traditionally said to have "lost contact with reality."

World, behavioral world, and self-in-world. Charlie Brown's world is also hi*s behavioral world*. He has a *status* in this world – a place or a position in the total scheme of things – and this self-in-world conception codifies his understanding of how he can and cannot behave. It codifies his unquestioned behavioral givens ("It's just a given that I could never be accepted by someone like her") and *options* ("My options in this world are such that I can only relate successfully to other Nothings"). Writ large, it codifies his behavioral possibilities and nonpossibilities in his world as he conceives it: "I'm a nothing and she's a something, *so I can't go over and have lunch with her.*"

In this connection, one can think of certain clinically relevant worlds and their behaviorial implications. A typical narcissistic world, for example, might be characterized as follows: "I am a unique and special person; I am superior to, unlike, and set apart from the common run of ordinary people; therefore I am entitled to, and insist upon, special treatment from them." One version of a psychopathic world can be expressed this way: "In this world, either you're a weak, gullible, expoitable sucker and get used and taken, or you're a knowing, superior con who understands the situation and how to exploit it; either you're a con or you're a sucker, and I intend to be a con." In the view of Karen Horney (1945), the world of a person beset with "basic anxiety" might be expressed this way: "I am alone, isolated and helpless in a potentially hostile world, and the strategy I have chosen in life is to move towards others by seeking the protection of stronger and more adequate individuals."

Change in world = personality change. In sum, every person has a world, appraises his or her position in that world, and behaves accordingly. Worlds tend to persist – that is, one does not as a rule see the world as a dangerous one today and a safe one tomorrow, or see oneself as alone and helpless today but loved and powerful tomorrow. As a result, people tend to behave accordingly *on an enduring basis*. Michael, for example, seeing the world as a dangerous place, withdraws, takes few chances, and engages in all manner of security operations. Observing these behavioral consistencies, others (as well as Michael himself) generate trait descriptions of him. He is said to be "cautious," "anxious," and/or "timid." Further, Michael exhibits, not just these traits, but a broader set of traits. He is also, for example, generous, sensitive, and considerate. It is this broader set of traits that constitutes what we refer to as his "personality."

Personality thus has its roots in the fact that people see their worlds in a certain way on an enduring basis, and behave accordingly. Personality *change*, then, has its roots in significant changes in the way a person sees the world. Charlie Brown comes to see himself as a Something, reappraises his eligibilities, and acts on his new sense of self-in-world. People who live and act in a dangerous world, or a contest world, or an eat-or-be-eaten world, sometimes have experiences that cause radical revisions in their world views ("epiphanies" or "conversion experiences"), and as a result come to act in radically new ways. Others, observing them, remark that they have "changed personalities" or that they are "changed persons."

Change in world = change in consciousness. A person's consciousness is always "consciousness *as*" (Jeffrey, 1998; Putman, 1981; 1990; 1998). That is to say, people always experience the world from some status or position in the world, and this position significantly determines the nature of their experience. The visitor to a foreign country has a very different experience – a very different consciousness – depending on whether he or she is there as a tourist, a missionary, or a spy; he or she experiences *as* a tourist, *as* a missionary, or *as* a spy. Two observers of the winning goal in an athletic competition, one an ardent fan of the victorious team and the other of the losing team, have a very different experience of that single event, even if they are seated next to each other and the physical stimuli impinging upon them are virtually identical; one experiences the proverbial "thrill of victory," the other the "agony of defeat." Charlie Brown's experience of the world, should he assign himself the status of a Something, will be quite different from when he was a nothing. Thus, the clinician who can bring about important changes in a person's world will correspondingly bring about changes in that person's very consciousness.

Problematic worlds and impossible worlds. Above, the connection was drawn between a person's world, including his or her conception of the place of self within that world, and that person's behavior potential. A person's world may be said to be "problematic" when it unnecessarily limits that person's ability to behave. Charlie Brown, an ineligible Nothing in a world of worthy Somethings, cannot approach the red-haired girl. Our Horneyan individual, alone and helpless in a potentially hostile world, is unable to go out into that world and participate fully. Instead, she feels compelled to withdraw from emotional and physical dangers to a position of safety. A paranoid individual, perceiving self-directed conspiracies and machinations all about, is unable to enter into trusting relationships.

The extreme case of a problematic world may be termed an "impossible world." Such a world is one that renders behavior impossible, that reduces the person's behavior potential to zero or virtually zero. Such persons are immobilized by their current formulation of how the world is, their own position in the world, or (usually) some combination of the above.

Clinical Application: World Reconstruction Therapy

"Worlds are not once and forever things," in the words of Mary Roberts (1985, p. 21). Since individuals construct them in the first place, they can reconstruct them. In world-reconstruction-focused psychotherapy, the task of the therapist is threefold. It is, first of all, to assess the client's world, conceived here as coming to an understanding, both empathic and objective, of this world and of the client's perceived position in it. Second, it is to figure out why and in what respects this world is problematic or impossible for the client. Third, and most critically, it is to help the client *reconstruct* his or her world in such a way that it is no longer problematic or impossible. Therapy here is fundamentally about having a conversation for change, and creating other relevant experiences, that enable the client to *reconstruct* a viable – and ideally a rich and meaningful – world. The remainder of this chapter presents clinical examples that illustrate practical implications of this approach.

Loss and Grief

In William Worden's excellent 2002 analysis of the four tasks that must be accomplished in order to resolve a loss successfully, his first task is that of "accepting the reality of the loss." The task here is essentially that of recognizing, in the fullest possible way, that the deceased individual is gone and that one will never see, touch, talk to, or otherwise have a relationship with that individual again. The failure at this task is simply denial – the refusal or inability to acknowledge the reality of the loss of this person.

In Worden's schema, the mourner cannot successfully complete the other three tasks involved in mourning unless he or she first accomplishes this task. If an individual has not first recognized a loss, it stands to reason that he or she cannot (a) work through to the pain of grief, (b) adjust to an environment in which the deceased is missing, or (c) emotionally relocate the deceased and move on with life.

Thinking in terms of worlds introduces an element into the analysis of grief that, so far as I have been able to determine, is not recognized by any other account of the process of grieving. A person cannot accomplish Worden's task 1, the full recognition of the loss, unless *a further precondition* is met: The individual suffering the loss must, at least to some minimal degree, be able to envision a viable world for himself or herself without the presence of the deceased (or other lost person). If the individual cannot envision such a world – if a world without the deceased is simply *unthinkable* for the individual – then that individual will not be able to see the world as it is: one from which the deceased is gone. All of this is in keeping with the assertion of Peter Ossorio that "A person will not see the world in such a way that it leaves him (or her) no place." (1998, p. 24).

From a clinical standpoint, introducing this additional element enriches our understanding of what is involved in grief and its successful resolution. First of all, it includes a critical element missing from current accounts. Further, it provides an important lead for the many cases in which the client is in denial, and thus is unable to accomplish Worden's first task. It says to us as therapists assisting clients with grief issues that, rather than pound away at the client's denial in an attempt to get him or her to see the reality of the loss, we would do well instead to back up and explore where the loss would leave the individual. The objective in doing so is not merely to explore, but in the course of doing so to expand that world in such a way that the loss at issue becomes a thinkable one, and thus one that the grieving individual can recognize. The following case example illustrates the clinical application of this idea.

A grieving mother. Julia, a married, 37 year old woman, had lost her 7 year old daughter Katie 18 months before intake. In that interval she had been racked with pain over the death. Upon assessment, I noted that Julia's pain did not actually arise from grief, but rather from a desperate struggle to keep from fully recognizing and acknowledging the loss of her daughter. Julia told me that she had kept Katie's room untouched from the day of her loss, repeatedly went there and "talked to her," and explicitly stated that, if she really let herself acknowledge that Katie was gone forever, she believed she would "go crazy." In addition, she strenuously suppressed any thought or image that would remind her of her loss. Clearly, Julia remained in denial and had been unsuccessful at accomplishing Worden's first and most essential task, that of fully recognizing the loss.

In addressing this state of affairs, rather than trying immediately to break down Julia's denial, I inititiated a conversation in which I attempted to get her to envision a meaningful world for herself without her daughter. Informing her that I first needed to understand her total situation before we could proceed, I asked her to describe her remaining world. I asked about such things as her marriage, her relationship with her remaining child, her work, her friendships, and what activities she had previously found meaningful and enjoyable. The idea was to tease out, dwell on, elaborate, and bring home to her the many ways in which her remaining world could in the future be meaningful and satisfying to her. In essence, I was calling on her to create a vision of how she could conduct her life in which she could derive meaning and satisfaction. Tentatively, since she only logically acknowledged the death of her daughter, I was also calling on her to see how she might derive some meaning from her loss (such as by advocating for better school crossings, which were involved in her daughter's death).

Having explored all these questions at some length, evoking from her a rather extensive vision of a possible world without her daughter, I undertook the more traditional work of having her confront the reality of her loss. I asked her explicitly to imagine such things as her daughter's face, what she looked like in her school uniform, and particularly poignant moments she had shared with her daughter. At the same time, I urged her to look directly at the fact that she would never see or talk to or touch or *in any way be* with this lovely young child again. This proved wrenchingly painful. However, within two sessions Julia was able to attain considerable recognition of her daughter's loss, marked lessening of her intense pain, and significant letting-go of her ongoing relationship with her (such as her conversations in the daughter's bedroom). In subsequent sessions in which we pursued this strategy, as well as Worden's further tasks, Julia ultimately resolved her grief. The initial strategy of getting her to envision a viable world for herself after the loss of her daughter seemed key to helping her finally recognize and grieve her terrible loss.

PTSD: Trauma and Impossible Worlds

In Post-Traumatic Stress Disorder, a traumatic event (or series of events) very suddenly ushers an individual into a new world. Typically, the individual has inhabited a world marked for the most part by safety, predictability, and controllability. In this world, the possibility of catastrophes such as a car suddenly smashing into you, a date assaulting you sexually, or flood waters rushing in on you seemed remote. Most people have the sense that, if such events threatened, they could probably handle it – get out of the way in time, verbally or physically deal with the threatening rapist, and so forth. The old world was habitable, viable, comfortably livable. With an implicit sense of trust in it, a person could largely forget about potential threats and safely focus attention on the many relationships, duties, pastimes, joys, and sorrows occupying center stage in one's world.

The traumatic event radically transforms all this. Like the announcement of an imminent atomic attack, it takes over the person's world and thrusts everything else to the periphery. This transformed world, in contrast with the old one, is unsafe, unpredictable, and uncontrollable. The individual has drawn the "lesson" from the traumatic event that catastrophic things *can* happen to him or her, and that when they do, there may be no way to see them coming in time, and no way to master or prevail over their overwhelming power. Further, the lesson is that this is the way the world *is*, not *was* for a now past, brief, anomalous moment in time. The traumatized person has the sense, not of something past, but of something present. A repetition of the cataclysmic event feels like an ever present danger.

In such a world, the classical symptoms of PTSD make eminent sense. The person is (a) chronically anxious, (b) ever-expecting and on guard against a repetition of the traumatic event, (c) trying strenuously to avoid situations reminiscent of the original traumatic one, (d) struggling to suppress all thoughts of the original event but experiencing a "return of the suppressed" in which he or she is compelled to relive the event in dreams, reveries, and even flashbacks, and (e) so consumed by the ever present life and death danger that nothing else matters, leaving the individual emotionally numb to all of life's other joys and sorrows. The post-traumatic world is extremely difficult to live in, and many who experience it retreat into a highly circumscribed, safety dominated, restricted existence.

In the case of the PTSD victim, the primary obstacle to recovery is the ongoing presence in the person's world of something that, like atomic holocaust, has the status of the *unthinkable* and *unfaceable*. The return of that flood or rape or sexual betrayal or automobile crash is felt to be so horrific, so utterly beyond facing, that one cannot even think about it, much less face it once again. Further, when something in a person's world constitutes such an enormous, unthinkable threat, it creates a sense of ever-present danger. By way of analogy, consider a messenger boy who is given a million dollars in an envelope and instructed to transport it on his bicycle to a bank across town. No matter how slight he might logically estimate the danger to be, and how completely sure he is that neither he nor anyone else has ever been robbed along this route, the magnitude of what is at stake – *of what must not happen at all costs* (losing that million dollars) – creates a powerful sense of present threat. Likewise, when the unthinkable has entered a post-traumatic client's world, logic and probabilities matter little; what is at stake is the possible reoccurrence of the unthinkable and unfaceable, and in such a circumstance, constant fear and vigilance are called for.

From a status dynamic point of view, then, the central therapeutic goal becomes that of removing this unthinkable element from the individual's world, and the preferred means for accomplishing this end is, to paraphrase Freud, that of *making the unthinkable thinkable*. Procedurally, a now substantial body of research suggests that the most effective therapies for Post-Trauamatic Stress Disorder are the various exposure therapies. In these therapies, the individual re-experiences the traumatic event by relating it to another warm, empathic, understanding person (also known as "disclosure"), and/or by reliving the event by imagining it, perhaps many times, in a safe, controlled and established manner. The following case illustrates both the successful use of exposure therapy and its compatibility with the status dynamic approach.

Unsafe at any speed. Anne, a 60 year old single woman employed as an executive secretary, came to therapy in the aftermath of an automobile crash. Driving with her sister one day, she stopped at a stop sign, and then proceeded into the intersection. A car approaching from her right at considerable speed smashed into the rear of her car, causing it to spin wildly out of control. Immediately after the accident, Anne and her sister, both unhurt, were shaken but seemed fine. The following day, however, Anne experienced the first of what proved to be a series of panic attacks, and in the ensuing days and weeks things became progressively worse. She began to experience intrusive, highly anxiety provoking memories of the crash, and became involved in a desperate struggle to avoid these through distraction and thought stopping. Anne slowly but surely retreated from driving, became more and more reluctant to leave the safety of her home, and at the peak of her illness was substantially confined to her home beset with chronic anxiety and struggles with intrusive thoughts.

The centerpiece of psychotherapy with Anne was the exposure therapy known as "Eye Movement Desensitization and Reprocessing" (EMDR) originated by Francine Shapiro (2001). Employing this procedure, I asked Anne to bring to mind all at once her total sensory experience of the event, as well as her emotions and thoughts while undergoing it. While she was doing so, I waved my hand back and forth before her eyes for a brief period, asked her to relate her experience of this, discussed it briefly, and then repeated this sequence a substantial number of times. This intervention, coupled with a considerable amount of discussion during each session, brought about a very significant improvement in Anne's condition. At termination, she was able to leave her home, drive, revisit the site of her accident, and return to work.

In employing this EMDR exposure technique with Anne, my rationale was not based on the traditionally favored theories of either (a) eye movement-brain event interactions, or (b) extinction of a classical conditioned response. With respect to the first of these, the empirically demonstrated fact that all exposure therapies work about as well as one another, but most do not involve eye movements, suggests that any theory that centers around such movements is incorrect in accounting for changes obtained with this method. With respect to the second rationale, classical conditioning theory requires, for the extinction of a conditioned response, that the conditioned stimulus (e.g., Pavlov's bell) be made to occur repeatedly in the absence of the unconditioned stimulus (e.g., Pavlov's meat powder). But this is not at all what occurs in EMDR and other exposure therapies. In these therapies, *both* the conditioned and unconditioned stimuli (in Anne's case, driving a car and being in an accident) are repeatedly presented in conjunction with each other. Thus, extinction cannot explain the favorable outcomes that these therapies often produce.

The rationale for Anne's therapy was in terms of worlds and the introduction into Anne's world of something that she had come to regard as utterly unthinkable and unfaceable. The constant message to her throughout the therapy was: "You *can* look at what happened to you. It was horrible, but it is not unthinkable or unfaceable. You do not have to run from it night and day, and you do not need to curtail your life for fear of a recurrence. You can go out and live in a world where this once happened, and where there is a remote chance that it could happen again. Moreover, you *must* look at it. You must face it down, because what is happening to you now is what happens when you don't."

I conveyed this message (which is highly consistent with the *practice*, though not the traditional *theories* of exposure therapy) over and over, implicitly and explicitly, in numerous communications to Anne. Some examples:

- "It is safe here. You can look at it here in a safe, controlled, scientifically tested way, and you will see how it will lose its power, how you will become more and more desensitized to it, as we go forward."
- "You *did* deal with it once. In fact, you dealt with it extemely well when it actually happened. You could deal with it again if worse came to worse, and by some remote chance it happened again."
- "It's good to talk about and relive this. When your mind brings it back, that's exactly what it's trying to get you to do: to relive it, to learn that you can face it, and thereby to overcome it."
- "Native American shamans teach that, if something is

frightening you in your dreams, turn and face it down, and you will conquer it. It's the same here."

Overall, in one way or another, the goal of this ultimately successful therapy was to get Anne to take a part of her world that she had given the status of the unthinkable and unfaceable, and to change its status to "something that was horrific, but that I *can* look at, *can* face, *can* relocate in the past, and whose remote possibility of repetition I can go out and face in my life."

Meaningless Worlds

Victor Frankl once asserted that "Some worlds are worth living in; some are not" (1969, p. 8). Concerned essentially with humankind's search for meaning, he meant by this that some people's worlds are such that action within them is stripped of much of the meaning that it might otherwise have, and they wind up leading their lives beset with a painful sense of meaninglessness.

What are the requirements for a person's world to be found meaningful? While an extensive answer to this question is beyond the scope of this book, consider the implications of the following suicide note articulating the meaningless world from which its writer subsequently eliminated himself: "Imagine a happy group of morons who are engaged in work. They are carrying bricks in an open field. As soon as they have stacked all the bricks at one end of the field, they proceed to transport them to the opposite end. This continues without stop, and every day of every year they are busy doing the same thing. One day one of the morons stops long enough to ask himself what he is doing. He wonders what purpose there is in carrying the bricks. And from that point on, he is not quite as content with his occupation as he had been before. I am the moron who wonders why he is carrying the bricks" (from Yalom, 1980, p. 419). This man's precise complaint is that, in the world as he finds it, he can find no *instrumental, intrinsic, or spiritual significance*. His actions, analogized as a pointless carrying of bricks back and forth, accomplish no valued utilitarian end that he can detect. They possess no intrinsic value for him. And, unlike Camus' Sisyphus, of whom his description is reminiscent, he can find no spiritual or transcendant value in the activity that might enable him to endure or even to affirm it. The "absurd," the quintessence of meaninglessness, is precisely what is generated when instrumental, intrinsic, and spiritual value are missing from human behavior.

In addition to the above absurd world, a second well-known version of a meaningless world lies in various reductionistic scientific views that have filtered down into the belief systems of many educated persons, particularly those with a scientific bent. One relatively common version of such a world view is the following: "Human beings are nothing but a very recent, utterly accidental, and therefore rather insignificant product of physical processes that began with the big bang. They are, like all of their evolutionary forebears, organisms – essentially, organic machines that operate according to deterministic physical laws. That is the end of the matter: all talk of this ephemeral life form finding a valid foundation for its self-invented moral rules, having freedom and responsibility, deserving acclaim or blame, or living in some relation to a supreme being is metaphysical nonsense without any scientific foundation."

To cite a third and final type of world view that is conducive to meaninglessness, there are a number of personal outlooks, often referred to as "cynical," that reduce individuals' ability to find their worlds meaningful. These would include outlooks such as "Everybody, myself included, no matter how altruistic or loving or unselfish they may appear, is essentially acting out of self-interest" and "It's a jungle out there, it's survival of the fittest, it's a world where the basic operative principle is 'eat or be eaten'."

All the above world views, whatever their level of intellectual sophistication, reduce the value of human actions. Everyone, from Mother Teresa to Stalin, is doing what physiochemical or sociobiological or environmental forces dictate, what's best for "number one," or what in an absurd or reductionistic world must be regarded as morally equivalent. In such world views, many of the values or significances that might otherwise be found in a given behavior can no longer be found – for example, that the behavior was done out of love or altruism, was virtuous, exhibited courage, or represented the doing of God's will.

For the most part, world views such as these are not irrational in the customary sense that they embody distorted logic or fail to square with empirical evidence. Because of this, the suggested therapeutic approach is not the traditional cognitive therapeutic one of trying to disconfirm the client's world view as illogical or empirically unsupported. It is, rather, to listen carefully to such a view, to convey an understanding of it, and to affirm its inherent logic and sense. Having done so, the subsequent tack is to point out to the client that his or her position is not that of a helpless victim doomed to see the world in the only possible way that it can be seen. It is instead the much more powerful one of *author* or *constructor* of a world. Unfortunately, in a world where there are many viable world views, and no uniquely true or correct one, the client has constructed one that permits little in the way of meaning. Status dyamically, proceeding from this position of leverage – of author and not victim – the therapist can show the client that he or she can make a choice to reconstruct this world view in a way that is equally or more realistic, but that permits the derivation of far greater meaning. Should the client elect to do so, the therapist may then assist in this process.

****

As psychotherapists, we are presented with many opportunities to assist our clients in reconstructing their worlds. This is a key aspect of the status dynamic approach. While the examples chosen in this chapter focussed on problems of grief, Post-Trauamatic Stress Disorder, and meaninglessness, it should be stressed that the range of world reconstruction-based applications is far greater than this. You will find additional examples in the remaining chapters of this book, as well as in the excellent 1985 work on this subject by Mary Roberts (see reference section).

Chapter 4
Changing Self-concepts

"Status takes precedence over fact."

--Peter Ossorio (1982/98, p. 18)

Sandy, a young college woman, had long appraised herself as "slow" intellectually. She had acquired this view of herself in part because she was the youngest child in a family of highly educated and rather accomplished individuals. Since the family placed a great premium on being intelligent, being "slow" was a very core element in her self-concept, and a very painful one that had caused her to set her sights in life rather low. Growing up, Sandy was always a bit behind everyone else in her family since she was two years younger than her next oldest sibling. The family treated her as the cute, amusing but somewhat dim "baby of the family," and she came in this way to adopt such a view of herself. Sandy, however, had completed grade school with almost all A's, and graduated from a very competitive high school with a 3.5 grade point average. When she entered therapy, she was again carrying a 3.5 average while taking a demanding science curriculum at a large state university.

In therapy, I asked Sandy how she squared all the evidence from her scholastic career with her view of herself as unintelligent. How could she continue to look at the many "A" and "B" grades from teachers in demanding courses and still regard herself in this way? In teasing out the answer to this question, Sandy revealed the many ways in which she preserved her conception of herself as "slow" in the face of what would seem overwhelmingly contradictory evidence. Confronted with an "A" grade, for example, her primary explanation was along the lines of the old saying about genius being more a matter of perspiration than of inspiration: "Isn't it amazing what an unintelligent person like me can do if I work hard enough!" On other occasions, she explained away her success on grounds that she had been lucky, that the professor was not very demanding, that she had fortunately studied just the right things, and/or that it was her roommate's help that got her through. Finally, when Sandy occasionally did receive a bad evaluation, she viewed this simply as confirmation of her lack of intelligence. The net result was that her self-assigned status, "unintelligent person," had remained remarkably intact despite what, on the traditional view of the self-concept as an informational summary of perceived facts about oneself, seemed to constitute massive evidence to the contrary.

In Sandy's case, I worked to change this core aspect of her self-concept in the following ways:

- Having personally assigned her the status of "intelligent person," I educated her regarding the nature of statuses, how they work, and especially why they tend to remain unchanged in the face of what would seem to be contradictory evidence.

- I helped her to see how "unintelligent" was essentially a status or place she had been assigned in her family of origin. She saw that the facts strongly suggested that this place was assigned more on the basis of her necessarily lagging position in her family than on anything factual about her intellectual abilities.

- In collaboration with Sandy, we teased out the picture described above of how she unwittingly preserved her status as an unintelligent person by holding fast to it as an unquestioned given, while interpreting all events to make them consistent with it.

- I assigned her some homework in order to place her in a position of power that she already occupied but didn't realize, that of a self status assigner who was continually interpreting facts to fit her status. Having made a list on an index card of all the specific ways in which she preserved her self-concept in the face of inconsistent facts, I gave her this card. Then, I instructed her to go out that week and, every time she did something that seemed to require significant intelligence, to take the card out and say to herself, "It's just a given that I am an unintelligent person; this seeming discrepancy can be explained away in the following manner...", and then to check off one or more of the discounting explanations listed on the card. In implementing this exercise, Sandy was forced to consciously and deliberately occupy the position of a proactive self appraiser who was preserving a negative status by systematically discounting a great deal of evidence. Operating from this position, she found herself increasingly unable to support her previous modes of self appraisal, as well as her old conclusions about herself. In the end, she was able to assign to herself a new status: "intelligent person."

In this case, it should be underscored, the core intervention was not the classical cognitive one of evaluating a belief in light of empirical evidence. In fact, it was taken as an obvious given from the outset that facts such as achieving an A in college level organic chemistry were inconsistent with a lack of intelligence, and this matter was never even discussed. Instead, the core strategy consisted in (a) personally assigning Sandy the status of "intelligent," (b) educating her in how status works to preserve negative labels, (c) showing her how "unintelligent" functioned as a status in her thinking about herself, and (d) getting her to actively assume the position of a status assigner who was discounting her considerable accomplishments to fit a preconceived label, and who had a choice in whether or not to continue doing so.

With Sandy's case in mind, this chapter presents a status dynamic formulation of the self-concept and of self-concept change that differs considerably from traditional mainstream views. Let's start by looking at precisely what the self-concept is.

Nature of the Self-Concept

In the status dynamic approach, an individual's self-concept is conceived as that individual's summary formulation of his or her status. This conception differs significantly from traditional ones in which the self-concept is universally considered to be a kind of organized informational summary of perceived facts about oneself, including such things as one's traits, social roles, values, interests, and personal history. In essence, the traditional view of self-concept is a fact-based answer to the question: "Who am I?"

A helpful means for making the transition from this traditional view to the status dynamic view is to consider an analogy. Suppose that we have a chess board set up, the pieces arrayed in a midgame situation, and we are explaining to a child what a knight is. In doing so, it is very unlikely that we would use an informational summary approach, which would include telling her such things as that our knights were made of onyx, weighed 2 ounces, were forty years old, and were made in Mexico. Rather, we would tell her what the knight's place or position was in the total scheme of things. Thus, we would describe what a knight's relationship is to the other pieces in the game: its ability to capture them, block their movements, move in relation to them only in a certain distinctive fashion, and so forth. Further, looking at any given knight's position relative to other pieces in the game situation displayed, we would help her to understand its current strategic importance. The crucial point here is that our thinking about what it is to be a knight is quintessentially relational or positional in nature. When we have completed our description, what we have given our child is a summary formulation of the knight's *status* – its overall place in the scheme of things – not an informational summary of many different kinds of facts about knights.

Returning from chess pieces to persons, the status dynamic view maintains that the self-concept is most usefully identified, not with an organized summary of myriad perceived facts about oneself, but with one's summary formulation of one's status. That is to say, it is one's overall conception of one's place or position in relation to all of the elements in one's world, including oneself. If you again briefly recall Charlie Brown's dilemma on the playground, you'll remember that he can't initiate a relationship with the little red haired girl because, as he puts it, "I'm a Nothing and she's a Something." In this example, Charlie provides us with a simplified illustration of the self-concept as a summary formulation of one's status ("Nothing" existing in a world comprised of "Somethings" and "Nothings"), and illustrates how what is fundamental about self-concepts is not that they are informational summaries of myriad facts about oneself, but that they place one somewhere in the scheme of things.

Self-concept Equals Perceived Behavioral Possibilities

By virtue of it being a summary formulation of one's status, a person's self-concept is also a summary formulation of his or her perceived behavioral possibilities, and of the limits on these. To pursue our chess analogy, when we have given our young student a summary formulation of the status of a given knight by virtue both of its powers as a knight and its current position relative to other pieces in the game, we have simultaneously formulated everything that this piece can and cannot do at this point in the game. When Charlie Brown makes a summary appraisal of his own status as that of a "Nothing in a world of Somethings," we see that he has simultaneously appraised his behavioral possibilities and the limits on these. When Sandy makes an appraisal of her own status as that of an "unintelligent person" in a world where, based on her family's indoctrination, intelligence is the all-important key to worth and opportunity, we see that she has simultaneously appraised her vocational and social status possibilities and the limits on them.

How do our self-concepts limit our behavioral possibilities? First, as captured in Charlie Brown's lament, once we assign ourselves certain statuses, we believe that we are ineligible for many valued forms of life participation. As you may remember from chapter 2, when clients assign themselves statuses such as "unlovable," "irrational," "inadequate," "incompetent," "worthless," or "inferior," in doing so, they declare themselves ineligible for various forms of participation in life. If Shaun believes himself to be "unlovable," for example, he sees himself as ineligible for, or unworthy of, the love of other persons. If Gail believes herself "irrational," she perceives herself as incapable of rendering logical, well-grounded judgments and decisions, an ineligibility that has vast behavioral implications.

A second limitation imposed by a person's self-concept is captured well in the expression, "I could never do that and still be me." Here, people are bound by their self-concepts in such a way that, being who they take themselves to be, a contemplated action is unthinkable as something they would or could do. In their minds, it would so violate who they are that, should they do it, they could no longer take themselves to be the same person, but would be forced to see themselves as different – and usually much lesser – persons. In many ways, this constraint serves as a force for social good since for most people antisocial acts such as child abuse or murder are "unthinkable" or "something I just could never see myself doing." However, at other times, this constraint proves debilitating in people's lives when crucially needed actions such as leaving a destructive relationship, or standing up for themselves in an assertive and forceful manner, are unthinkable for them.

Finally, persons will "read" the world in ways that are in keeping with their self-concepts. For them, this will seem "just the way the world is," and this reading of the world often proves both limiting and destructive to our clients. For example, one of my clients, Dave, when urged to look at some positive things about himself, responded that, "You don't seem to understand; the deep-down bedrock truth about me is that I am a complete and utter a–hole." From Dave's point of view, given his self-concept, my favorable comments could only be read as a case of my "not getting it." Further, given this self-concept, praise from his employees was always read as ill-motivated deceitful flattery, and minor criticisms from his wife as emotional abandonments. To have a self-concept is, in the end, not just to have a certain appraisal of oneself – it is to live in a certain world.

Self-concept Influences How People Think They Should Behave

An old expression in the American culture has to do with people "knowing their place." Often used with reference to individuals in devalued social positions, the notion here is that people who know their place understand their position in the social scheme of things, know what it calls for in terms of behavior towards others, and behave accordingly. The expression "knowing one's place" captures well certain behavioral implications of the self-concept when viewed as one's summary formulation of one's place or status. As therapists, we observe that clients whose self-concept is that of "lowly nothing" will often express this by behaving towards others in ways that are self-effacing, deferential, nonassertive, and even servile. In contrast, other clients, whose conception of themselves is that they are "special persons," will frequently express this with behavior that is arrogant, demanding, presumptuous, condescending, and heedless of the rights and desires of others.

An important special case of the self-concept determining how it is appropriate to act concerns how individuals behave toward themselves. Depending on the statuses they assign to themselves, they might judge it appropriate to do such things as continually criticize themselves for their many failings, disregard their own rights and desires, doubt the soundness of their judgments, engage in continual efforts to transform themselves from unacceptable human beings into acceptable ones, or even in extreme cases, execute themselves.

Self-concept Resists Empirical Disconfirmation

A well-documented fact about the self-concept is that it possesses a curious resistance to change, even in the face of what clearly seem to be disconfirming facts. Sandy continues to believe herself to be intellectually inferior despite what others view as compelling evidence to the contrary, and does so even when this evidence consists of facts that she herself recognizes as both positive and true. A man believes himself selfish despite the many factual counterinstances posed by his reassuring friends. World renowned musicians and actors, despite years of glowing reviews from critics, continue to believe that they are inadequate, and will surely fail and disgrace themselves the next time they step on stage.

What does the status dynamic view have to say about this? In short, the self-concept is impervious to seemingly contradictory facts because, as discussed in the previous section, it does not function as an informational entity at all, but instead functions as a positional one. Consider this: so long as my assignment of a position to someone does not change, there is no way for any new fact to disconfirm my belief that he or she occupies that position. In such a situation, there are no disconfirming facts. For example, if I know that Tom's position on the baseball team is pitcher, no fact that I discover about his behavior or accomplishments as a player will disconfirm my belief that he is a pitcher. The most that any such fact – for example, that he bats .350, or that he does not possess a particularly strong throwing arm – might do is to inform me of something that I find quite surprising for someone in his position. Moving in a more clinical direction, if I am a bigot, and I have assigned to some outgroup the status of "inferior," I might accurately perceive the impressive accomplishments of members of that outgroup but wind up thinking only that "some of them are surprisingly talented...but of course they're still inferior." Finally, if my self-assigned status (self-concept) is that I am an uncaring person, and I perform an act that appears caring and thoughtful – say, I send a condolence card to a friend who has lost a loved one – for me, this will not count as evidence that I am a caring person. Rather, I will tend to regard it as an uncharacteristic (or questionably motivated, or merely socially obligatory) thing for an uncaring person like me to do. In the end, the important general truth here is that contained in the quote at the beginning of this chapter: "Status takes precedence over fact" (Ossorio 1982/98, p. 18).

Further Barriers to Self-concept Change
In most cases, like Sandy's, the origins of self-concept problems lie in the statuses that families, peers, school personnel, and others assigned to clients when they were very young. Parents, for example, may have labeled the child as "bad through and through," "mommy and daddy's perfect angel," or "our emotionally disturbed child," and these status assignments may have varied widely in the degree to which they miscast the child. Moreover, each of these statuses carried with it certain ways that the child was to be regarded and treated, as well as a place or a part in the family drama that the child was to carry out.

For the most part, children tend to unreflectively accept the statuses that important others have assigned them. Unfortunately, by the time they have acquired the level of observational and critical powers that might enable them to evaluate and question these statuses, they already have well-established self-concepts. Thus, for a considerable period of time, they have been operating from within an unquestioned formulation of self-in-relation-to-world that determined how they saw themselves and their worlds, how they acted, how they restricted themselves, how they viewed events, and more. Furthermore, they have with some frequency incorporated certain attributes into their self-concepts such as "irrational," "stupid," or "screwed up" that have caused them to disqualify themselves as persons who are competent to rethink and redecide their status. Finally, in many cases, they might have found themselves unable to effectively dispute or otherwise change the family's or spouse's view of them. For all of these reasons, the effects of parents and others assigning negative statuses to children can be both devastating and permanent.

Despite this discouraging picture, clients nonetheless occupy a position of power, greater or lesser depending on the individual, from which to reconsider and change their self-concepts. The critical fact here is that, in the last analysis, the self-concept is by definition self-assigned – it is one's own conception of oneself. While individuals may in most cases have had little say in its formation, they are now in every case persons who are currently accepting the statuses assigned by others, and assigning them to themselves. As implied in Eleanor Roosevelt's famous assertion that "no one can make you feel inferior without your consent," we all retain the critical power, at times precious small, to effectively dissent from and to revise the debilitating statuses that have been assigned to us by others.

This conception of the self-concept conveys a number of important advantages over traditional informational summary accounts. Foremost among these are the following.

Parsimonious Account of Resistance to Change

As noted previously, abundant empirical evidence supports the contention that the self-concept is resistant to change in the face of seemingly disconfirming empirical evidence. Traditionally, the way out of dilemmas involving inconsistent factual information has been to posit ego-defensive mechanisms that result in persons either failing to register negative evidence about themselves at all, or distorting such evidence so as to render it non-injurious to self. Such accounts encounter several serious problems:

- Many of them involve positing unobservable and highly questionable censoring mechanisms that somehow review all facts, decide if their level of threat to the self is tolerable, and if it is not, repress or distort them.
- All such accounts have difficulty accomodating the frequent,

highly clinically significant cases where the disconfirming facts in question are positive, fully recognized, and acknowledged as true by the individual ("Yes, I know that I spend countless hours doing things for my children, husband, and others, but I still feel like I am a selfish, narcissistic person.")

• All such accounts require a commitment to a basic view of people as inherently irrational – that is, as creatures who by their very nature are determined to deny or distort reality in light of their needs. This position is enormously undermining to the whole enterprise of therapy (and for that matter, science) as a rational enterprise, since presumably therapists (and scientists), as persons, are not exempt from such reality-distorting inevitabilities.

The formulation of self-concept as a summary formulation of one's status explains the phenomenon of resistance to change more parsimoniously, does so without positing unobservable mental mechanisms, easily accomodates the cases (such as Sandy's) where such resistance occurs in the face of positive and fully recognized information, and accomplishes all of this without any commitment to a view of persons as inherently irrational.

Ties Together a Wide Range of Phenomena
The status dynamic account of the self-concept ties together a wide variety of observed empirical phenomena. As documented above, it explains why individuals restrict their behavioral possibilities, how they decide which actions are appropriate, how they view the world, how the self-concept limits change, and why self-concepts resist change in the face of seemingly disconfirming evidence. From a pragmatic clinical standpoint, these many linkages bring home an important point for the efficient and powerful conduct of psychotherapy: the self-concept is a "linchpin" factor. That is, it is a single explanatory element lying at the heart of a wide array of factors crucial to the quality of persons' lives (for more on this, see chapter 5). Thus, if clients can make changes in their self-concepts, they may therefore expect to experience changes in these many other factors, and thus a profound improvement in the overall quality of their lives. With these thoughts in mind, let us consider some therapeutic interventions that my collegues and I have

employed to good effect for many years.

Psychotherapy: Changing Self-Concepts

In the status dynamic approach to helping clients alter their self-concepts, as typified in Sandy's case, change is fundamentally about enabling them to move out of the limiting self-assigned statuses that are the source of their problems, and assigning themselves new statuses that convey far more behavior potential. To accomplish this we create a two-person community with our clients, assign certain statuses to them, and treat them with the utmost consistency as persons who have those statuses. In essence, while we often employ traditional means such as cognitive restructuring, insight conveyance, or behavior rehearsal, our primary means of achieving change is to place clients in relational positions that are incompatible with the ones embodied in their self-concepts.

Assessing, Reformulating, and Assigning the New Status

In the status dynamic approach, the fundamental task of assessment is to determine the nature of the client's presenting difficulty and, if relevant, the problematic self-concept that is at the root of it. In Sandy's case, we assess her initial concerns with depression, low self-esteem, and pessimism about her future, and establish how these are rooted in her conception of herself as an unintelligent person barred from full participation in a world where superior intelligence is the key to everything good.

Having assessed these matters, our next task as therapists is that of reformulating who the client is – of reformulating the client's status within his or her world. In the ideal case, this reformulation would possess the following characteristics:

- It would be realistic. It would be consistent with the facts regarding the client's actual position in the scheme of things. It would not be some implausible view that the client would find incredible or, should he or she accept it, find impossible to carry off in the real social world.

- It would expand the client's behavior potential. That is, it would take a form such that previous limitations would be diminished and new possibilities and alternatives would be opened up.
- It would, in the best of cases, alter the significance of the client's whole life (see case of Paul, "the catcher in the rye", below).

Note the contrast here to other therapeutic approaches. In many of them, clients must change their behavior and/or cognitions first before success can be attributed. The premise of such therapies is in essence, "Well, you are quite unsuccessful now, but through our therapy I believe you can some day do much better." From a status dynamic point of view, it is better to provide clients with empowering *actualities* – for example, a more positive view of who they are already – than it is to give them only hope for better possibilities.

This approach is fairly straightforward in cases where the therapist assesses the situation and sees the client from the outset in very status-enhancing ways. However, obviously, there are times when the therapist surveys the situation and finds that the client's status is a far less salutary one. To illustrate, think of Dickens' *A Christmas Carol* and the three ghosts who placed Ebenezer Scrooge in a position that forced him to see a very unflattering picture of who he had become. In such cases, the therapist, like the three ghosts, might need to assign a less socially desirable status, but one calculated to make a significant difference in the client's behavior potential (see case of TJ, "the con man", below). This unflattering status assignment, further, would be intended as transitional, a stop on the way to a new and better position in the world and a correspondingly better conception of self.

Finally, having arrived at a reformulation of the client's status, the fundamental strategy of the status dynamic therapist is to assign the client this status, and to steadfastly treat him or her accordingly. The therapist engages in the powerful tactic of putting the client in a new position, and treating him or her as an occupant of that position with the utmost consistency possible. Expressed verbally, it is as if the therapist is saying to the client: "This is who you are, and this is who I will treat you as being." Obviously, as with any approach, it is critically important for therapists to watch for any reactions or further information from the client that would indicate that their assessments and/or interventions have been misguided, and to make appropriate adjustments if needed.

To further convey how the status dynamic approach works in modifying clients' self-concepts, let's examine two more cases.

The con man. TJ, a man in his late forties, initially requested therapy with Jim because he had been having multiple affairs during most of his 30 year marriage. He despised himself for this, but did not think he could stop. In addition to this primary concern, TJ reported others. In his job, he was in trouble much of the time because he repeatedly informed his superiors that he was completing work when in fact he was not. He was constantly in debt because he acted the role of "big spender" and "man of means" with others, when in fact he was often on the verge of bankruptcy. He had a long history of alcohol abuse, but had been sober for several years when he entered therapy. Basically, TJ lived his life with smoke and mirrors and was always just a few steps away from one crisis or another, all of his own making.

At the time of intake, TJ's basic conception of himself was that he was a Nobody masquerading as a Somebody. Beneath his public displays of bravura, he saw himself as a weak man who in his countless affairs, pretenses at being a man of means, lies to his superiors, financial crises, and abuse of alcohol had failed at everything in his life.

A man of relatively small stature who grew up in a tough neighborhood, TJ had always yearned to be a "big man" on the street. In his neighborhood, the model of a big man was the "made man," or professional criminal who played by his own rules, cared about little, and was afraid of nothing. While TJ did not have the size and strength to make it as a physical tough, he achieved status in his neighborhood by becoming a consummate con man. He became someone who could talk people into doing what he wanted, get women to feel sorry for him and lure them to his bed, and always get around doing what he was supposed to do. He was very good at getting out of any trouble he might create, often by having his parents, and later his wife, clean up any messes he made.

In the past, other therapists had told TJ what was wrong with his behavior, but TJ seldom went back to them for more than 2 or 3 sessions. Not wanting to repeat this unsuccessful strategy, Jim, using a status dynamic approach, assigned TJ a new status, one that both fit the central facts of TJ's life and that cast him in certain important respects as both successful and powerful. However, given the largely unsavory details of TJ's life, this status was akin to the negative one assigned by the three ghosts to Ebenezer Scrooge. Like the ghosts Jim's hope was that this new status would spur positive changes in TJ and thus prove to be only transitional.

Jim's initial message to TJ was this: "The way I see it, you have succeeded very well in becoming exactly who you always wanted to be: a successful con man who can deceive others into giving him what he wants. You've become a man who can get all the women he wants, who derives enormous satisfactions from presenting himself as a big man and a big spender, who doesn't have to play by the rules like everyone else, who can successfully avoid the tedious, day-to-day stuff that ordinary people have to put up with – and who at the end of the day can almost always get away with it. You've been very successful at becoming exactly who you wanted to be, so why give it up unless you find something better?"

TJ readily accepted this status assignment, this portrayal of who he was. However, the portrayal spoke to and satisfied only one side of his ambivalence, the part of him that had always wanted to be a successful criminal. It did not satisfy the side that experienced emptiness, self-hatred, and worthlessness for having destroyed his marriage, family, and career. The one side being satisfied and the other unsatisfied, it did not take TJ long to experience his acute dissatisfactions with the status quo. He soon began to ask questions like, "Well, if it makes so much sense for me to do all these things, how come I don't enjoy them anymore?" and "How come nothing and nobody means anything to me?" Jim then began to show TJ that the most he could ever accomplish if he pursued his lifelong agenda was to become a better con man, and no matter how good a con man he became, he was likely to find it provided limited satisfaction and little significance once he proved he could get away with it. Having given TJ the status of "successful con man," Jim in essence caused him to experience the emptiness of his place in the world.

If TJ wanted enjoyment and significance in his life, the answer was conceptually simple: give up being a con man and be authentic. In other words, give up impersonating someone with something to offer and be someone with something to offer. At this point, Jim, noting certain other qualities and motivations in TJ, assigned him a second and more accrediting status: that of someone who did have something genuine and valuable to offer. Not surprisingly, it took Jim a good deal of time to get TJ to a place where he could see that he actually had something of value to offer others, and that he had more behavior potential through being authentic than through being a con man. While the details of this effort are beyond the space limitations of the present chapter, two examples convey a sense of the final phase of the therapy.

TJ knew a good deal about computers and was something of a graphics expert. In the course of therapy, Jim made it a point to ask for TJ's advice about a number of computer problems. In doing so, his objective was to assign TJ the status of "computer expert and consultant with a genuine, high quality contribution to make." In response, TJ offered his help freely and was visibly pleased that he could help his therapist. Jim then focused on what it was like for TJ to be in a relationship in which people could and would depend on him.

A second significant interaction had to do with the many lies TJ told to his family and his employer to cover up his misdeeds. In one session, Jim said to him, "You usually don't have to cover things up if you have clean hands." For some reason, this expression struck a chord with TJ and became a motto for him in many of his subsequent dealings with the world. While he struggled with the idea, it became an important part of his formulation of who he was becoming: a person who played it straight and did not have to lie because he kept his hands clean.

Over the course of several years, TJ developed a radically different self-concept, that of someone who had something genuine and valuable to offer others, and who therefore could succeed without being a con man. As this conception developed, he ventured into a wide range of new positions in the world. He obtained a new job in which he had to produce at a high level on a regular basis. He worked hard to develop a love relationship with his wife, even though that meant dealing with the results of many years of betrayal and mistrust. He was able to regain the respect of his children. At last report, he and his wife were making significant strides in their relationship. He has performed exceptionally well in his job. Recently, his difficulty in managing financial responsibilities resulted in a fairly significant crisis, but he took full responsiblity for the crisis and managed to find a way to deal with it on his own.

The catcher in the rye. Paul, a 42-year-old administrator of a large child care agency, came to Laurie for family therapy for problems surrounding the anorexia of his eldest daughter, age 17. In the course of the family work, Paul, feeling extremely distraught by events, requested some individual sessions with Laurie. In these sessions, he reported a very painful sense that he had been a "failure in life." To substantiate this, he related that he had been subjected to very emotionally abusive treatment growing up, had had an extremely painful childhood, and now suffered greatly from a sense of terrible failure as a parent. Despite the fact that he had vowed to himself early on that his children would never suffer the way he had, he believed that he had damaged his daughter by his hovering, overconcerned, and overprotective ways, and had failed to protect her from terrible emotional pain.

Paul's summary formulation of his status, his self-concept, was "failure in life." However, Laurie did not see him this way at all. Instead, she found that Paul brought spontaneously to her mind the image of J.D. Salinger's *Catcher in the Rye*. Acting on this appraisal, she told Paul about the image, and asked him if he was familiar with Salinger's book. When Paul responded that he was not, Laurie shared this story with him: "The catcher in the rye was a fellow who one day came upon thousands of little children playing in a field of rye. At one end of this field, however, there was a steep and dangerous cliff, and there were no other adults around. Seeing this dangerous situation, the man became deeply concerned about the safety of the children, and stationed himself by the edge of the cliff. Whenever any of the children came too close to the edge, he would catch them and gently lead them back to a place where they could resume playing in safety. As you were talking about your life, Paul, this is the image that kept coming into my mind. You remind me very much of the catcher in the rye. You suffered terribly when you were a child and you basically made it your life's mission to protect children from having to go through the kinds of things and the kinds of pain that you went through. To do this, you went into the child care field, and have been successful in achieving many good things on behalf of children in trouble. Furthermore, with your own children, it is very clear to me that you have gone to the 'ends of the earth' to protect them from going through what you went through, and have succeeded in making them feel tremendously loved and valued. Even though things have not turned out completely as you had hoped yet, still it is very clear to me that this has been your mission, you have succeeded at it in many, many ways, and you are still working on it in coming into family therapy today."

This image, and the personal accreditation conveyed with it, touched a deep chord in Paul. Upon hearing it, he broke down and wept for about five minutes. Most importantly, he accepted this new and far more accrediting status assignment, this radical reappraisal of himself, his life mission, and his human value. Furthermore, Laurie, who genuinely saw Paul in the manner described, continued to regard and treat him in keeping with the image. While much work remained to be done in the family therapy, Paul was able to continue his efforts with considerably less depression and a vastly improved sense of well-being, optimism, and drive.

In this case, Laurie attempted an unusually brief, but nonetheless ambitious accreditation – in effect, a reframing (or rewriting) of the client's personal history and of the significance of his entire life. Her basic message to Paul was, "This is who you are, this is who you always have been, and it is very far from being a failure." When such an accrediting status assignment is accurately conceived, compellingly presented, and acted upon consistently by the therapist, the effects are often, as they were in this case, profound.

****

In this chapter, I have presented a status dynamic formulation of the self-concept and of self-concept change. I believe, and I hope I have succeeded in demonstrating, that individuals' self-concepts function as self-assigned statuses, and not as informational summaries. Most importantly, I hope that I have shown that viewing them in this way provides some new and better ideas about how to help our clients to improve their self-concepts.

Chapter 5
Individual Case Formulation

"There is nothing so practical as a good theory."
--Kurt Lewin

"In each separate case it is necessary to create,
as it were, a theory and technique made for the
occasion without trying to carry over this individual
solution to the next case."
--Otto Rank

The ideal clinical assessment would culminate in the construction of an empirically grounded, comprehensive *individual case formulation* that organizes all of the key facts of a case around a "linchpin." That is, it organizes them around some factor that not only integrates all of the information obtained, but in doing so also identifies the core state of affairs from which all of the client's difficulties issue. Further, it does so in such a way that the clinician and the client can use this formulation in matters such as selecting a therapeutic focus, identifying an optimum therapeutic goal, and generating effective forms of intervention. Most importantly, it allows the clinician to focus therapeutically on that one factor whose improvement would have the greatest positive impact on the client's overall problems. The status dynamic approach offers a way to achieve these desirable goals. Let's see how it works.

Individual Case Formulations

In the optimum case, an individual case formulation would embody the characteristics listed in this section. In relating these, I shall for simplicity's sake speak as if the client were always an individual, but everything that will be said applies equally to couples and families.

Further, since the central concern here is with a desired *product* of assessment and not with its methods, I will not be concerned with the means (interviews, observations, tests, etc.) that might be used to gather information.

The Approach Organizes Facts Around a "Linchpin"

In the typical clinical case, in addition to presenting a problem (or problems), the client virtually always provides an abundance of further information. This information might include items about his or her emotional state, current situation, personal history, world view, perceptions of self and others, goals, expectations, and more. In some cases, clients have organized this information into a personal theory or formulation of the problem, but this formulation has not allowed them to find a successful solution. In other cases, clients have not organized the data into any sort of coherent cognitive package, and thus experience a confusing jumble that has rendered focussed, effective remedial action difficult or even impossible. For example, they have not organized the data into causal sequences (e.g., "This fact A about me results in facts B and C about me"). Or, they have not distinguished those factors that are important and relevant from those that are neither. Frequently, they have overlooked relevant items of information that are critical for solving their problems, such as important maladaptive beliefs or personal behavior that creates interpersonal difficulties. In any event, whether clients' views be confused or defective in these or some other way, they stand badly in need of a new formulation of the problem that will enable them to resolve it. The following case illustrates such a situation.

The hopeless one. Curt, a 37-year-old owner of a successful small business, possessed little beyond some fragmented mini-theories regarding what lay behind his host of highly distressing presenting concerns. I will attempt to capture something of his confusion by simply relaying the basic items of information he provided at intake in roughly the order that he related them.

Curt began by stating that he had been "desperately unhappy" for as long as he could remember, but was sustained by a meagre hope that his depression would lift. He had had fleeting thoughts of suicide at various times in his life, but had never come close to an actual attempt. He reported chronic anxiety, as well as chronic worries over matters such as losing his business or his health. He wondered aloud if he might somehow "want to be unhappy" or "be driven to be unhappy." Curt stated that, objectively, he seemed to have a good life, since he had a successful business, a devoted wife, and ample financial resources. He then went on to report that "I am a shit, and I live in constant dread that I will be exposed as such . . . a fraud." He related that he was haunted continually by the question "Who am I?" and that this left him "desperate for some image to crawl into." He said he was a "bullshitter" who "snowed" his customers into purchasing work of mediocre quality, and felt guilty about this. He saw himself as "undisciplined," "stupid," "untalented," and "pathetic." Finally, he said, he craved the applause of his employees, and could only feel good about himself and enjoy a sense of identity when he had put in a long hard day of productive work and received acclaim from them. Even when this happened, the following day he felt like these accomplishments counted for nothing. Despite considerable intelligence, Curt had never been able to understand how this crazy quilt of complaints fit together, much less what he could do to rid himself of them.

My job as the assessing clinician was to organize this mass of data into a usable unity. I needed to sort the relevant from the irrelevant, to discern what was cause and what effect, to bring items of information into the equation that Curt had perhaps not even considered, and to do whatever else it took to discover how everything fit together. In the end, and here the present conception diverges from many others, my job was to discern the crucial *linchpin* at the heart of everything. Ideally, that is, I would discover some factor that would not only organize all of the information obtained, but in doing so would identify the core state of affairs from which all of Curt's difficulties issued. Determining that kind of organizing source at the heart of any client's difficulties will have the status of an *empirical hypothesis* or *theory*, and its adequacy will be determined by how well it fits all the important facts of the case and how fruitful it proves as a generator of successful therapeutic interventions.

This idea of linchpin factors might seem to violate the widely held contention that human problems have multiple causes, and that they therefore do not lend themselves to explanation by some single factor. However, it should be clarified, the concept of a linchpin is not that of a single cause or influence acting in isolation. Rather, it is a concept having to do with what lies at the center of multiple states of affairs – *a common pathway* as it were between prior influences and current consequences. A linchpin, as the metaphor implies, is what holds these factors together. If removed, it might cause them – most importantly, the destructive consequences – to fall apart.

In Curt's case, the linchpin that seemed best to organize and explain all the data had to do with his mode of self-governance. The term I employed to characterize this mode was that of an "overseer," an image that has been used in the past to capture the central issues in obsessive-compulsive personality disorder. In his position or status of overseer to himself, Curt had instituted a regime of self-governance entailing certain modes of self-direction and self-criticism. In brief, his mode of self-direction was self-coercion, and his primary operative "commandments" were (a) "Thou shalt be engaged in constructive, productive, utilitarian work activity at all times; any other activity is a frivolous and sterile waste of time" and (b) "Thou shalt be the best, and be perfect, in everything you do."

When he felt, as he usually did, that he had violated these commandments, Curt's mode of self-criticism involved heavy resort to highly degrading labels ("undisciplined," "stupid," "unlovable") and excessive harshness. His constant negation of any value in his own behavior or in himself arising from his ceaseless self-criticism left him unable to conceive any positive overall image of who he was, a state of affairs that he characterized as a "poor sense of identity." In sum, Curt's regime of self-governance created (a) continual perceptions of personal defect and failure, (b) constant anxiety both that he would be "found out" and that he was ill-equipped to meet life's challenges, (c) a poor sense of identity, and (d) deep depression and despair that he could ever become an acceptable human being.

The foremost advantage of identifying a linchpin is that it permits the therapist to target what might be termed the *biggest ripple factor* in the case. This is the factor that, should it change for the better, would have the greatest positive impact on all the client's difficulties and on his or her life in general. In Curt's case, for example, if he can alter his characteristic mode of self-governance in more effective and humane directions, we would expect to notice positive effects in his depressive mood, self-esteem, hopelessness, anxiety, chronic worries, and sense of identity.

In contrast, when the facts of the case permit such a unification, but we as therapists fail to identify an organizing state of affairs at the center of the client's problems, the danger becomes that of needlessly pursuing change in a piecemeal fashion. For example, in Curt's case, if I hadn't found a common link, I might have then regarded him as a "multi-problem case" and adopted a strategy of taking his list of complaints, prioritizing them, and pursuing them one at a time.

As you can see, determining and therapeutically addressing linchpin factors results in a much greater efficiency in therapy, but this efficiency is not achieved at the cost of superficiality. We do the client the inestimable service of getting to the heart of the matter.

The Approach Targets Factors Amenable to Intervention

Not all truths are created equal. Despite the promise of the linchpin approach, a therapist could posit the existence of a linchpin factor for a case in such a way that the formulation might in essence be true, but not sufficiently useful from a therapeutic standpoint. For example, such a formulation might link all the facts of a case to some event(s) in the client's past (e.g., child abuse or being the child of an alcoholic), some global personality trait (e.g., obsessive-compulsiveness), some mental disorder (e.g., generalized anxiety disorder), or some state of affairs not amenable to direct intervention (e.g., a "symbiotic tie to the mother" or "weak ego boundaries"). The point here is not that such facts and descriptions are without value or importance. It is that they are not suitable as *ultimate* formulations because they are not framed in terms of factors (a) that are currently maintaining the client's dysfunctional state, and (b) that are directly amenable to therapeutic intervention.

The fundamental purpose of assessment is to guide us toward interventions that will resolve our client's problems. Thus, the ultimate product of assessment, the individual case formulation, would ideally be framed in terms that permit ready translation into effective therapeutic action. For example, in Curt's case, I hypothesized that at the core of all of his problems and concerns was his current mode of self-governance. This mode of self-governance comprised certain self-directed critical behaviors. Such behaviors can be changed. It further comprised certain self-created and self-imposed rules and standards. Such rules and standards can be examined and, if found wanting, changed or rescinded. Finally, it comprised certain undergirding beliefs, for example, "I must treat myself this way to achieve excellence; anything less and I will lapse into complacent mediocrity." Such beliefs can be evaluated as to their soundness, and modified. Thus, the linchpin element in Curt's case, summarized as an "overseer regime," is explicitly formulated in terms of factors that are highly amenable to therapeutic intervention.

The Approach Enables Beneficial Use by the Client

Once we have constructed a linchpin formulation, we can share it with our clients to their considerable benefit. The formulation, first of all, can organize clients' thinking about their problems. Rather than being handicapped by a defective personal formulation of their problems, or feeling enmeshed in a bewildering maze of emotions, perceptions, and self-accusations, the client can identify one central maintaining factor. Second, the client can discern in this central factor a focal point toward which he or she should direct energies for change. Rather than struggling on multiple fronts or not knowing where to attack their problems, clients can pinpoint the place where they can most effectively target their change efforts. Third, the ideal formulation would fulfill a basic status dynamic agenda of placing clients in positions of power. Rather than locating the root of the problem in some factor that might seem incomprehensible and/or beyond their control – for example, their history, character, or possession of a mental disorder – it locates it in something they are doing and/or thinking, and so in principle could cease to do or think. Thus, it diminishes the tremendous fear, helplessness, and hopelessness that attend clients' beliefs that they are mentally ill or otherwise helpless in the face of their problems.

For these reasons, I recommend that therapists share linchpin case formulations with their clients. Further, when negotiating a therapeutic contract, I recommend that therapist and client adopt the linchpin element as the focus of their collaborative efforts. In the case of Curt, for example, I did share the the overseer formulation with him. And, as I'd hoped, it (a) diminished considerably his confusion and his helplessness about his multiple problems, (b) identified the specific behaviors, rules, and beliefs that he needed to alter, and (c) showed him where best to focus his efforts to change. Finally, as the core element in our therapeutic contract, it became the explicit focus of collaborative efforts that ultimately helped him revise his basic mode of self-management, and with this its many painful and debilitating consequences.

Guidelines for Developing Individual Case Formulations

There are certain human activities where we can follow a routine, step-by-step procedure, and a certain outcome is largely guaranteed. Following a recipe from a cookbook or directions for how to put a new bicycle together are examples of this. However, many other human activities do not lend themselves to such an approach. Writing a novel, designing a software program, or figuring out how to address a delicate interpersonal issue come to mind here. In them, we are forced back on a basic strategy in which, first being clear on what we want to achieve, we use our relevant knowledge and competence flexibly and creatively to try to achieve it.

As you may have guessed, creating linchpin case formlations falls into the second category. There is no step-by-step formula that, followed on all occasions, will ensure a successful outcome. What I can provide here are some general guidelines for creating linchpin formulations that have proven helpful to me and my colleagues in the past.

1.Follow the "Detective Model" of Assessment

In creating clinical case formulations, the first step in the present approach, as in most approaches, is that of carefully ascertaining the important facts of the case. In the status dynamic approach, the clinician behaves like a *detective* who first determines the precise nature of the crime to be solved, and then uses this as a guide in determining what sorts of evidence are and are not relevant. On this "detective model," in contrast with assessment methods in which the information to be gathered is predetermined, the clinician begins by getting a very clear picture of the presenting concern. He or she then uses this picture to determine what kinds of facts are relevant to creating an explanatory account of the problem, and focusses efforts on gathering these facts. Such an approach streamlines the assessment process by minimizing time spent gathering extraneous information.

2. Don't Make Anything Up

In obtaining assessment information, a primary caution is not to admit anything into the clinical picture that is not grounded in the facts of the case. In response to this, you might think, "How obvious can you be!" While this caution is indeed obvious, I mention it because in my experience it is so frequently violated in clinical practice. For example, some clinicians will include factors such as "low self-esteem," "poor self-concept," "underlying anxiety," or "must have been abused as a child," in their case formulations without there being any evidence that such factors are actually present. It could indeed be true that such factors are at the root of some clients' problems, but as case formulators, it is incumbent on us to ground such attributions in the established facts of the case.

3. Develop the Facts into an Explanatory Account

The third basic element in erecting a case formulation is that of developing the facts obtained into a useful explanatory account of the client's difficulties. Here, two separate guidelines may be helpful.

The first of these involves *dropping the details and looking for the patterns that emerge*. That is, as the facts of the case unfold, the clinician de-emphasizes the details and seeks to detect broader patterns. For example, in Curt's case, I de-emphasized the myriad details of his complaints – his many degrading self-characterizations, painful emotions, life events, and more – even as I noted that through it all there ran a theme of debilitating self-governance. Thus, I devoted primary attention to establishing the precise nature of this self-governing pattern, and this proved to be the linchpin for all of his other difficulties. To cite a second example, a young male client, Harry, reported a series of romantic relationships whose dissolution both confused and disturbed him. Rather than focusing on the details of these romances, I discerned what might be termed a "Pygmalion pattern" that ran through all of them. Harry repeatedly chose naive, dependent women and successfully enlisted them in a process of changing themselves under his guidance. However, in his behavior lay the seeds of his ultimate failure. When these women changed, they no longer found the guru-pupil arrangement congenial, and abandoned him. With experience, most clinicians acquire a large repertoire of clinically significant patterns, and this knowledge base is extremely helpful in detecting the larger patterns in specific cases.

The second method for developing the facts of a case into a useful explanatory account involves *assimilating these facts to known explanatory forms*. Some of the more well known of such forms are associated with prominent psychological theories. These include: "People tend to act in ways that they expect to be successful in securing desired states of affairs"; "A person will take the world to be as he or she has found it to be"; and "Helplessness elicits passivity elicits helplessness." Other, less widely promulgated, but nonetheless valuable, explanatory forms include "Coercion elicits resistance," "Provocation elicits hostility," and "Status takes precedence over fact."

4. Check, Implement, and Revise if Indicated

Once we arrive at an initial case formulation, it is important to re-check it by entertaining several questions: Is the formulation consistent with the facts we have observed? Does it account for all of them? Does it provide a good fit with the pattern or explanation we are thinking is the linchpin? Does it suggest specific interventions that have a good prospect for success? If the formulation proves deficient in any of these ways, we must revise it. If it does not appear to be deficient, the next step is to implement the formulation through clinical interventions. Finally, once we have the opportunity to observe the results of such interventions, we can use these results to maintain or revise the initial formulation.

In the last analysis, generating clinically useful and powerful individual case formulations is not, as noted above, a matter of following some pre-established, step-by-step procedure that guarantees success. Instead, it is a matter of *competence*. Like any other competence, it can be developed by most clinicians who make its acquisition a personal goal and who work hard over time to search for integrating linchpin factors in their clinical assessments.

A Second Case Illustration: The Fire Stopper

Fran, an 18 year old freshman at a large state university, came to therapy with a presenting concern of compulsive behavior. The only child of two very caring but overprotective ranchers in eastern Colorado, she had come to the university to pursue a career as a consultant to ranchers on commodity price fluctuations. Her ambition, in her own words, was "to keep them from being wiped out." Soon after arriving on campus, Fran had begun to experience a strong compulsion to make sure that all of the electrical switches in her dorm room were turned off whenever she left. Attempts to overcome this problem by simply making herself leave the switches on resulted in intense anxiety. Probed about reasons for her behavior, Fran stated that she was afraid that, should she leave a switch on, the dorm's electrical circuits would overheat and cause an electrical fire. Asked about fuses and circuit breakers, she stated that she was fully aware of the nature of these protective devices, but that this knowledge made no difference. At the conclusion of her intake session, Fran expressed concern about the tendency of psychotherapists to place the blame for problems on their clients' parents. Noting that "this is my problem and not theirs," she admonished me to "keep my parents out of this."

After making little progress in our first three sessions, I asked Fran to recount her fears of what would happen if she left an electrical switch on. She reiterated that she feared an electrical fire. I then asked her to take the matter further and to tell me what would happen as a consequence.

"Well, the dormitory would burn down," she replied.

"Okay, and what would happen then?"

"Well, I don't know why I think this, but somehow I feel like the university would not have full insurance coverage."

"And then...?"

"My parents would have to make good the balance."

"And then...?"

"They would lose their ranch and wind up financially ruined and disgraced because of my behavior."

Thus, from this unusual exchange emerged a chain of obsessional thoughts having to do with her parents' ruination and disgrace, as well as a clarification that the function of her behavior was, however magically, "to keep them from being wiped out."

Pursuing this matter further, I hypothesized that an individual who was having persistent fantasies about her parents' destruction was likely a person who harbored some anger toward them. In light of Fran's warning to keep her parents out of the therapy, I explored this hypothesis very cautiously. It emerged over the next few sessions that Fran indeed harbored enormous anger toward her parents, and that, while she suppressed it, she was quite aware of this anger. She related that she felt stifled and smothered by her parents' overprotective ways. Further, she believed that they exerted constant pressure on her to shine in the world so as to shed glory on them. Finally, it emerged that Fran had an extraordinary reluctance to broach even the slightest of issues with her parents for fear of hurting them, and so had accumulated a vast store of unresolved issues and grievances over the years.

Thus, I hypothesized that the linchpin in this case was Fran's suppressed anger toward her parents. Having its roots in a host of unresolved grievances coupled with a radical inability to address and resolve these, her mounting anger manifested itself in the form of obsessional fantasies of their financial destruction and disgrace. However, since Fran also loved her parents and wished to protect them, she recoiled from these frightening fantasies and undertook strong measures to prevent their realization by turning off electrical switches. The hypothesis of anger as the linchpin factor, then, ties together a plethora of facts about the presence of unresolved grievances, Fran's inability to address these, the content of her obsessions, the content of her compulsion, and the overprotective, conflict-avoidant family environment in which her symptoms emerged.

Based on this linchpin formulation, I targeted therapeutic efforts toward helping Fran to (a) become aware of her anger as the central difficulty, (b) identify the unresolved issues that provoked this anger, and (c) become able to address and negotiate these issues with her parents in constructive ways. Despite some initial reluctance, Fran proved quite able to accomplish all these things. Further, far from being devastated when Fran raised issues with them, her parents were willing and able to discuss them, and a number of very constructive family dialogues took place. When she returned after Christmas break, Fran reported tremendous progress with her family effort and a complete absence of all obsessive-compulsive difficulties. At a six month follow-up, she remained free of symptoms.

In this case, then, identifying a current, central, problem-maintaining element, and modifying this element, resulted in a strong ripple effect. Fran's obsessions and compulsions were eliminated. She became far more competent at the core life skill of identifying and constructively addressing issues in intimate relationships. Her relationship to her parents improved. And, finally, Fran's family took a very important step away from their longstanding implicit rule that potentially divisive issues must never be addressed openly

Relationships to Other Approaches to Assessment

The DSM-IV Approach

Perhaps the most widely practiced approach to clinical assessment today is that promulgated by the American Psychiatric Association in its *Diagnostic and Statistical Manual of Mental Disorders*, Fourth Edition ("DSM-IV"). In this approach, one assembles an overall clinical picture based on information pertinent to five different areas or "axes." These areas have to do with the presence or absence of (a) a mental disorder (for example, paranoid schizophrenia or Post-Trauamatic Stress Disorder); (b) a personality disorder or mental retardation; (c) a general medical condition; and (d) psychosocial or environmental problems (for example, a recent divorce or job loss). Finally, it includes (e) a global assessment of the client's general level of functioning. In essence, the mental disorder typically constitutes the focal problem in this approach, while the remaining factors represent either causal factors (e.g., a medical condition or recent critical life event) that bear on the focal disorder, or contextual factors within which this disorder exists (e.g., the presence of a personality disorder or of a low general level of functioning).

As the case of Fran and her obsessive-compulsive disorder illustrates, use of DSM-IV diagnostic categories is compatible with the general approach advocated in this chapter. While these diagnostic entities do not fulfill the criteria for being regarded as linchpin factors, they can be regarded as an important subset of all problems that clients present.

However, the DSM approach to assessment and case formulation differs in important ways from the approach recommended in this chapter. Essentially, DSM-IV's axis methodology does not call for any of the characteristics cited above as constitutive of an optimal case formulation. First of all, it does not call for any attempt on the part of the assessing clinician to identify a central, problem-maintaining factor whose modification would provide a broad positive ripple effect. Second, it does not advocate that a clinical case formulation be framed in terms of factors that are amenable to intervention. Third and finally, it contains no recommendation that the formulation be sharable with the client as a means of (a) organizing the client's thinking, (b) clarifying where change efforts would best be targeted, or (c) placing the client in a position of power by framing the problem in terms of things that he or she is doing or thinking, and so in principle could cease to do or to think. Indeed, DSM case formulations largely fail in all of these respects.

In sum, what emerges here is a general picture in which there is no incompatibility between the use of DSM-IV mental disorder categories and the present approach. However, there is substantial incompatibility between its assessment and case formulation methodologies and those advocated in this chapter.

Other Related Approaches to Clinical Case Formulation

A few other authors have viewed case formulation in a manner similar to that of the linchpin approach. For example, Thomas Schact and his colleagues, employing a psychodynamically oriented interpersonal approach, stress the importance of determining in each case what they term the "dynamic focus." This is a repeated pattern of interpersonal behavior on the part of the client that the therapist perceives as central to the whole range of the client's problems. In the dynamic focus approach, the primary effort lies in helping the client to identify, understand, and ultimately modify this focal behavioral pattern. In a similar vein, Jacqueline Persons, operating within a cognitive framework, advocates a search for what she terms the "central underlying mechanism." This mechanism is a core belief (or "schema") that underlies all the emotional, behavioral, and cognitive difficulties one observes at the overt level, and the central therapeutic goal accordingly becomes the modification of this central belief. Finally, family systems therapists such as Salvador Minuchin characteristically search for, and seek to modify, repetitive interactional patterns (or "structures") that are both central and causal with respect to a wide range of problematic family phenomena.

The essential similarity between these approaches and the present one lies in their stress on the vital importance of determining central, organizing factors that are currently maintaining the problem and that are directly amenable to therapeutic intervention. The primary difference lies in the fact that each of these approaches needlessly restricts the range of what might constitute a central factor to their own theoretically preferred variables – Schact to interpersonal behavior, Persons to maladaptive cognitions, and Minuchin to familial structural patterns. In essence, each is *predetermining* the nature of the linchpin for every case. Such a restriction places an unnecessary, potentially problematic, and essentially a priori constraint on the enterprise of determining what is at the heart of our clients' problems. In contrast, the present approach advocates an open-ended, empirically-based search that, as the cases of Curt and Fran illustrate, might culminate in the determination that different kinds of factors are centrally operative in different cases.

Final Considerations

Linchpin Formulations Are Not Always Possible

At the outset of this chapter, I noted that I would be describing the characteristics of an *ideal* case formulation. Obviously, what is ideal cannot always be realized. In certain cases, for example, there could be two or more influential factors at work that cannot be integrated, and that will require separate attention. In other cases, as therapists, we will be limited by our own inability to discern integrating linchpin factors in the myriad facts of our cases.

No Uniquely Correct Linchpin

It is a general feature of the world that, for any given object, event, or state of affairs within it, there is no privileged, uniquely correct, "God's eye" description. Even something as simple as a rock may correctly be described as a "rock," "a piece of quartz," "a container of a geologic record," "a Newtonian object," and more. In the same way, it is possible that the same case material in the hands of two different competent clinicians might yield differing, but nonetheless cogent and effective individual case formulations.

****

When we can discover the presence of a central organizing linchpin in a given clinical case, we find ourselves in a significantly advantageous position. We can, by virtue of this, proceed in a highly efficient and economical, as opposed to piecemeal, fashion. Further, we are able to achieve this economy and efficiency without paying the price of superficiality, since we are getting to what might be termed "the heart of the matter" for our clients. Finally, we have in a linchpin formulation a central blueprint that provides a clear, constant goal for ourselves and our clients, a clarification for them of where their personal power for solving their problems lies, and a tremendous suggestiveness as to how we might proceed therapeutically to bring about important change.

Chapter 6
Policies in Status Dynamic Psychotherapy

A hallmark of status dynamic psychotherapy is adherence to a set of therapeutic *policies*. Policies are procedural guidelines for the effective conduct of therapy. Clients benefit from our adherence to these guidelines in the great majority of therapeutic situations. As with any general policy, specific circumstances always determine the best course; no policy applies in every situation.

An important topic in the field of psychotherapy has been the exploration of *common factors* – factors that transcend, and are critical to the success of, a wide variety of therapeutic approaches. The presence of an empathic, accepting therapeutic relationship is one well established common factor. The policies to be presented in this chapter can be regarded as common factors. Though generated in connection with status dynamic psychotherapy, they are not confined to it or to any single theoretical approach, and may be followed beneficially in connection with any approach.

The philosopher Ludwig Wittgenstein once stated that rather than saying anything new, his method was to "assemble *reminders* for a particular purpose." Some of the recommendations offered in this chapter can be thought of as "reminders" of things that many skilled therapists already know from their own experience or from the therapy literature. Other policies presented in this chapter will essentially be unique to status dynamic therapy. Whether unique to status dynamic therapy or not, however, all of these policies were originally assembled with only one criterion in mind: they represent principles of sound, effective therapeutic practice.

Some Key Therapeutic Policies

1. Deal With the Reality Basis of Emotions

Consider the following ultra-simple story: "A lion walks in the room...you feel scared...you take a happy pill...you don't feel scared anymore...the lion eats you." The contemporary mental health establishment, in its implicit policies, often amounts to a denial of the truth contained in this story. Some medical practitioners, in their exclusive reliance on drugs to eliminate states such as depression and anxiety, in effect follow a policy that says it is sufficient to chemically eliminate the client's painful feelings and not to bother with their source in the client's life or thinking. The practitioners of cathartic interventions encourage clients to deal with their painful emotions by expressing or "ventilating" them. These emotions, they believe, are like so much pressure that has built up in the pressure cooker and must be released lest the cooker explode – again, not a word about the lion. Finally, our cognitive modification colleagues recommend a core policy of modifying emotions by helping the client to reinterpret the reality that is causing the feeling. However, while this is very often helpful, it can be insufficient in situations where the reality clients are confronted with is *actually* devastating, such as child abuse, rape, incest, or devastating loss. In such situations one must ask: What good is a reframe in the face of a *real* hungry lion?

The point here is not that the above forms of intervention (as opposed to the implicit policies just stated) are without merit. The point, rather, is to say that a fuller and more adequate fundamental policy is needed here. "Deal with the reality basis of emotions" is such a policy. The position it rests on is that, first of all, emotions do not exist in a vacuum. They rest on perceptions or appraisals of reality. Fear, for example, rests on the appraisal that one is endangered, anger on the appraisal that one stands provoked, and sadness on the appraisal that one has suffered some loss or other misfortune. Such appraisals of reality could be well- or ill-founded; the lion before us could be real or a "paper lion."

The point is that we as clinicians must carefully investigate the perceptions or appraisals that provoke the client's problematic emotions. Should we discover that the emotion rests on a misperception or otherwise maladaptive interpretation of reality, we can use the traditional cognitive therapeutic approach of helping the client to modify such appraisals. Should we discover that the emotion rests on an accurate perception – for example, the client's marital situation is indeed abusive, or the personal loss has indeed drastically diminished the client's world – our task becomes that of assisting our client, in whatever way appropriate, to deal effectively with their problematic reality.

A final word about medications is perhaps in order before leaving this topic. In the present view, *merely* following a policy of narcotizing away one's pain with drugs is akin to disconnecting the flashing oil light in one's car, and doing nothing about the failing engine. Nevertheless, medications can serve a far more valid and valuable purpose. Consider a second simple story: "A lion walks in the room... you freeze in panic...you take a happy pill...you unfreeze...you run out the back door and escape the lion." At times, emotional states such as anxiety, depression, and grief are of such proportions that they are immobilizing. They prevent clients from doing what they need to do to deal with the reality basis of their emotions. In such circumstances, medications are often very helpful in reducing the emotional state and its paralyzing effects. However, in this instance, as the story suggests, they would ideally be part of a two-pronged strategy: get mobilized *and* do something about the lion.

2. Appeal to What Matters
"Use existing forces, don't oppose them."
--Buckminster Fuller

This policy advocates that therapeutic efforts in general be aligned with the client's existing motivations. Expressed negatively, it reminds us to avoid such actions as pursuing therapeutic agendas that are antithetical to the client's motivations, declaring clients "unmotivated," or appealing to motives that, however commendable, the client does not possess. Expressed positively, therapists are asked to assess the client's *existing* motivations, and subsequently frame all suggestions, reframes, and other messages so that they tap into them.

Thus, if Mary views morality as extremely important, this policy would suggest that her therapist is unlikely to succeed by urging her to "give up her irrational shoulds." Instead, her therapist is more likely to succeed by portraying Mary's problematic behavior as contrary to her existing moral values; new, potentially beneficial behavior can be portrayed as consistent with those values, representing "tough love" or "giving of herself." Similarly, clients who value such things as personal control, independence, integrity, uniqueness, or rationality can best be approached in ways that are consistent with these existing values, anand that utilize them. The use of this policy is illustrated in the following case:

The poopie contest. A young mother, Jill, brought her 4 year old son, Johnny, to the clinic. Johnny was about to enter kindergarten, and he had thus far refused to be toilet trained. Jill stated that she had "tried everything" to get her son to use the toilet, including verbal encouragement, various types of rewards for successful performance, time-out, punishment, and more. However, none of these had been successful, and she had become increasingly desperate as Johnny's entrance to kindergarten loomed.

After interviewing Jill, her therapist, Doug, asked to spend some time alone with Johnny in the playroom. He and Johnny talked and played together for an hour while Doug made numerous observations. Among these, he observed that Johnny was extremely competitive, and became quite upset if he experienced any setback whatsoever while playing a game. Seizing on this fact about Johnny, Doug made a recommendation to Jill.

The following morning, Jill woke Johnny as usual but delivered the following message to him in a gloating way: "I won the poopie contest." Johnny, bewildered, asked her what she was talking about. "I won the poopie contest," she reiterated, "I went poopie before you did today. Ha!" She immediately walked out of his room. The following morning, she repeated this message when she woke him. On the third morning, however, Johnny woke his mother and pronounced triumphantly, "I won the poopie contest today!" Jill feigned disappointment and told him that he was just lucky and that she would win the next day. Taking up the challenge, Johnny "defeated" his mother every day thereafter and in the bargain became toilet trained.

In this case, Doug and Jill appealed to what mattered to Johnny to bring about change. In Ericksonian terms, Johnny's preexisting motivation of competitiveness was *"utilized,"* that is, was brought into the service of bringing about a solution to the presenting concern. In Buckminster Fuller's words, the existing "force" was not "opposed," but "used."

3. Establish and Utilize the Client's Control

Many therapy clients hold *victim formulations* of their problems. That is, they conceive their problems in such a way that they see both their source and their resolution as lying outside their personal control. They might see the problem source as something *personal* such as their own emotions, limitations, irresistible impulses, personal history, nature, or mental illness, or as something *environmental* such as the actions, limitations, or character of another person. In either case, as "powerless victims" these clients cannot envision any actions they might take to bring about change and, in fact, have often come to therapy at a point where they have exhausted the behavioral options afforded by their formulations.

The therapeutic policy, "establish and utilize the client's control," advocates that in such cases we carefully investigate the client's portrayal of the problem to determine if he or she in fact occupies a position of control in relation to this problem. Should we discover that such a position exists, the policy recommends that we work to enable the client to recognize this position of control, to fully occupy (or "own") this position, and to utilize the power inherent in this position to bring about change.

Many client complaints have both a "perpetrator end" and a "victim end." Victim formulations result when clients are aware only of the victim end with its attendant emotional pain, low self-esteem, and other liabilities, but remain unaware of the perpetrator end of the problem, the end where they are actively *producing* some sort of unfortunate behavior that creates or maintains the problem. Being unaware of this perpetrator end results in clients feeling that this pain, low esteem, or other consequences are visited upon them and are outside their control. Essentially, they have left a critical part of the problem out of their formulation, and this has resulted in a failure to solve it.

Some examples: Many clients beset with painfully low self-esteem turn out to be the active perpetrators of destructive forms of self-criticism. Many individuals who experience behavioral paralysis and an inability to derive satisfactions in life are persons who, on the perpetrator end of things, coerce themselves excessively in ego-alien ways, and then rebel against their own oppressive regime of self-governance. And many clients experience themselves as victims of mistreatment from others, but fail to realize that these others are simply reacting to the clients' own behavior, often in the context of the sort of interactive "dance" much discussed by family systems therapists. An illustration of the policy of establishing and utilizing the client's control is found in the case of Kathy.

The rebel. A 23 year old graduate student, Kathy entered psychotherapy reporting that she suffered from bulimia, a diagnosis she had received from her previous therapist. Almost every day over the previous few years she had followed a pattern in which she restricted her food intake severely throughout the day, binged heavily on snack food in the evening, and then purged herself by vomiting. Despite an intense daily battle to resist her temptations to binge, she had been unable to stop, and entered therapy believing herself the victim of a mysterious and uncontrollable mental disorder.

In time, it became clear to me that Kathy's bulimia represented a rebellious act. The rebellion was against a self-governance regime in which, so that she could shine in the eyes of the world in every conceivable way – physically, morally, and educationally – she relentlessly denied herself food and coerced herself into many forms of activity that had little to do with her intrinsic loves and interests. In the evening, once she was alone, she rebelled against this self-imposed regime by overeating, and then felt compelled to undo the damage and to reinstate her coercive regime of self-improvement.

My strategy with Kathy was to shift her focus away from her view of herself as a powerless, craving binger to one in which she functioned as a high-power self-governor. I helped her to recognize and to focus, not on attempts to control her eating through will power, but on the highly problematic ways in which she directed her own life, and the consequences that ensued from this. Placing the focus of therapeutic efforts here, where she was the in-control perpetrator and not the victim, Kathy was able to change her pattern of self-governing behaviors in a far more reasonable and self-respecting way. With this change, since there was no longer anything to rebel against, she ceased her binging and purging. When I saw her for a six month follow-up session, I found that she had been able to maintain this change.

4. Don't Buy Victim Acts

Many clients, although they are not in the grips of a victim formulation of their problems, nonetheless *present themselves as victims* in order to evade responsibility, to gain sympathy, to get strategic leverage over others, or for other reasons. The policy, "Don't buy victim acts," advocates that we firmly but tactfully refuse to accept such self-presentations. Instead, it recommends that we make empathic contact with the person "behind the act" as it were – the person who feels the need to erect such a strategy of impersonation to deal with his or her life circumstances. Further, the policy advocates that we help these individuals to see what they are doing, to discuss their reasons for doing it, and to explore and adopt different solutions to the problems confronting them.

5. Avoid Generating Resistance

Peter Ossorio has given us the useful truism that, "If a person has a reason to do something, he will do it, unless he has a better reason not to" (assuming, of course, that he has the relevant abilities and the opportunity). For any given behavior, a person has reasons for and against engaging in that behavior. Eating the ice cream would be enjoyable, but it is fattening. Mowing the lawn would make the yard look better, but it is hot, tedious work. And so forth. From the vantage point of Ossorio's maxim, when therapy clients refuse or decline to engage in some behavior or to accept some alternative view of reality, the basic general diagnosis is this: As they see things, they have better reason not to.

Ideally, therapy would be resistance-free. Our clients, in the face of some potentially beneficial new behavior or view of reality, would have stronger reason to engage in this behavior or adopt this view than not to do so, and would proceed accordingly. The policy, "avoid generating resistance," advocates that to the extent possible, we conduct therapy so as to minimize the presence of resistance, that is, minimize the presence or salience of those "better reasons not to." How can we do so?

Many of the recommendations already made in this book, aside from their other benefits, serve to minimize resistance to our therapeutic agendas. We position ourselves on the client's side in an alliance when forming a therapeutic relationship, which gives the client reason to cooperate with us. We seek to understand and to convey this understanding to the client, becoming persons who speak to the client from a true understanding; we are thus more likely to be listened to and found credible. We offer portrayals of the client's reality that are realistic yet minimally degrading, rendering them easier to accept. In our reframes and suggestions for new behavior, we carefully align these with the client's existing motivations. Finally, we custom tailor our messages in terms of the client's favored language, metaphors, world views, and conceptions of the problem. Successful adherence to all of these recommendations greatly increases the likelihood that clients will be receptive to and cooperative with our inputs, and greatly reduces the likelihood of resistance.

In addition, a further way to keep resistance to a minimum is to avoid doing anything in the therapy hour that might be, or be seen as being, coercive toward the client. If our clients perceive us as coercive – that is, as applying pressure that they see as illegitimate – they will tend to resist this pressure. By illegitimate, I mean any pressure that the client sees as unfair, insensitive, threatening, authoritarian, presumptuous, or in any other way inappropriate.

Despite our best efforts, it is more or less inevitable that clients will resist at times. When we observe resistance, the present policy advocates that we attempt to ascertain its source and address it. Have we as therapists been coercive, or been seen as coercive? Have we miscalculated the client's reasons for and against something, and thereby suggested something that he or she has strong reason not to accept? Have we asked the client to take some action that is currently beyond his or her capabilities? If the answer might be yes, we must either act to remove ourselves from the position of perceived coercer and return to that of supportive and understanding ally, or else adjust our directives and messages in other relevant ways.

6. Respect Both Sides of the Client's Ambivalence
To be ambivalent about engaging in some behavior is to have

reasons for and against engaging in that behavior. In general, when ambivalent individuals fail to resolve their ambivalence and simply act on one side of it, their reasons for acting on the other side do not cease to exist; they become more salient. Consider the commonplace phenomenon, well known to automobile salespeople, of individuals who are ambivalent about buying a specific car. Frequently, those who buy the car, thereby satisfying the reasons on one side of their ambivalence, find themselves experiencing "buyer's remorse." That is, they experience a strong precoccupation with all the reasons why they should *not* have bought the car. In contrast, those who, before they can make up their mind, learn that the desired car has been sold and thus that they can no longer act on their reasons to buy it, frequently find themselves preoccupied with all the reasons why they *should* have bought it. The point here is that when a person acts on one side of an ambivalence, she satisfies her reasons for acting on this side, but she leaves unsatisfied a whole set of still existing reasons for acting on the other side, thus rendering them highly salient relative to the satisfied reasons.

As psychotherapists, we are often confronted with deeply conflicted, ambivalent clients. Should they leave their spouse or not? Quit drinking or not? Give up the affair or not? Cease their punitively self-critical approach to themselves or not? The policy, "Respect both sides of the client's ambivalence" recommends that as therapists we should (a) assess the client's reasons for and against important courses of action, (b) respect the fact that both sets represent important reasons for this individual, and (c) assist the client in arriving at a personal decision that is made with full consideration of their reasons on both sides of their conflict.

Stated negatively, the policy advocates that we should not, in the face of ambivalent clients, simply ignore certain of their reasons, in effect acting as if they don't exist, and encourage them to act on one side of their ambivalence. Doing so leaves something ignored that will undermine their ability to make firm, personally integrated decisions and to act on these decisions with comfort and conviction. For example, when Karen hears that Margaret, her client, is ambivalent about leaving her abusive spouse, she simply urges her to leave. What Karen can expect is that in response, Margaret will express the other side of her ambivalence (her reasons not to leave her spouse) in such forms as remaining on the fence with respect to her decision, resisting Karen, or, if she does leave her husband, having deep doubts and reservations about what she has done. Her ability to make an integrated personal decision and pursue a subsequent course of action with comfort and conviction will have been undermined by Karen's advice.

As noted at the start of this chapter, every policy comes with what amounts to an *"unless* clause": "Do this, unless you have a better reason not to." At times, therapeutic interests are well served by pushing one side of an ambivalence in order to deliberately heighten the saliency of the client's reasons on the other side. Thus, the therapist may encourage a client who is ambivalent about ceasing some problematic behavior to continue this behavior for a period of time and in certain prescribed ways. (You may recall that this was done in the case of Sharon, the "servant," in chapter one.) Doing so can help the client by making their reasons to cease this behavior more salient, in effect amplifying these reasons in their consciousness. Such a tactic, often referred to as "paradoxical," can be helpful when clients seem unable to recognize fully the downsides of their behavior and/or when they are resistant.

7. Assess What Matters

This policy advocates an approach to assessment already touched on in chapter 5, and I will review it only briefly here. There, I recommended that the clinician behave like a detective who first determines the precise nature of the crime to be solved, and then uses this as a guide to determining what sorts of evidence are and are not relevant. Using this detective model, the clinician begins by getting a clear picture of the presenting concern(s). He or she then uses this picture to determine what kinds of facts are relevant to creating an explanatory account of the problem, and focusses efforts on gathering these facts. This approach streamlines the assessment process by minimizing time spent gathering extraneous information. It contrasts with assessment methods in which the procedures employed and information sought are predetermined, ruling out practices such as *routinely* performing mental status examinations, giving questionnaires or projectives, administering intelligence tests, and asking about pre-selected topics. The policy advocates reserving the use of such procedures for situations in which the specifics of a case indicate that there is probable cause to warrant their use. For example, it might prove very difficult in certain cases to establish something important unless one administers an MMPI to the client.

8. Don't Expect the Client to be Somebody Else

This policy warns us first to guard against assuming that our favored interventions, no matter how well they have served us and others in the past, will be effective in every situation. Second, it advocates that, when clients fail to respond to these interventions, we do not conclude that there must be something wrong with them, that they must be "unmotivated," or "resistant," or "insufficiently psychologically minded." Rather than insisting that our clients should be responding to our treatments and blaming them when they don't, the policy recommends that we carefully assess what is unique about this individual client and how we might adjust our interventions to accomodate this uniqueness.

9. Choose Anger Interpretations Over Fear Interpretations

As therapists, we have choices in how we portray our clients to themselves. Depending on these portrayals, we give them reason to see themselves as more or less powerful, autonomous, and in control. And since people can more easily act from a position of power and control than they can from a position of powerlessness and victimhood, realistic portrayals that describe them in the latter way, if accepted, enhance their ability to act. A policy of choosing anger interpretations over fear interpretations is an important special case of this general truth. Let's look at an example.

A client, Tom, reports that his wife is engaging in a great deal of provoking behavior such as overspending to the point where she is causing severe financial strain on the family. Tom has never let her know how he feels about this. His therapist, Louise, might portray this in different ways. She might inform Tom that he has a "fear of asserting himself," an "inability to set limits," or "difficulty with getting in touch with and expressing his anger." Or she might portray Tom to himself as "punishing her by giving her the silent treatment," or as "emotionally rejecting her by refusing to communicate his genuine position and feelings on the matter." The former set of portrayals characterize the individual in a weaker position (fearful, unable, nonassertive). The latter characterize him as more powerful and more a perpetrator than a victim (punishing, rejecting, emotionally abandoning). Further, if he accepts the latter descriptions, he gains both an enhanced perception of personal power and a comparatively improved position from which to act. For example, it is generally easier to "cease punishing another" than to "overcome one's fears." Assuming a basic therapeutic relationship in which Tom feels that Louise is on his side, the status enhancing aspects of being described as powerful and in control will usually more than compensate for the pejorative elements in such descriptions.

10. Go First Where You Are Welcome

Almost all psychotherapists agree that one of our initial jobs is to establish an alliance with our clients in which we function as an accepting, supportive collaborator who is genuinely on their side. Not infrequently, however, clients present information during initial assessment that leads us to conclude that not only are they suffering and struggling to cope with difficult circumstances, but they are themselves the perpetrators of unfortunate behavior and/or the holders of quite unbecoming attitudes. In such circumstances, the policy "Go first where you are welcome," advocates that we intitiate treatment by focusing on clients' distress and complaints first, and only later take up the matter of how they themselves could be contributing to them. Thus, we would focus our early attention on listening carefully to clients' emotional suffering and personal dilemmas, conveying an empathic understanding of them, and thereby establishing both that we genuinely understand their point of view and that we are on their side. Later, once the alliance is established, we tactfully broach the matter of clients' contributions to their own problems. Clients, assured that we know, understand, and accept them, and that we are truly there for their benefit are far more likely both to disclose these aspects and to be responsive to our interventions.

11. If It Works, Don't Fix It

This policy advocates that, if we discern client characteristics, attitudes, or behaviors that are functional, we ought not to portray them to the client as problematic or pathological. While this point might seem obvious, it is frequently violated. For example, this sometimes happens when clients conduct themselves in ways that are not in conformity with a certain widespread ethos among therapists. Perhaps Bill never raises his voice in anger and addresses issues somewhat indirectly; nonetheless, the facts indicate that Bill's messages get across and that he is effective in his dealings with others. Perhaps Lisa uses humor to lighten problematic situations, but there is no indication that she fails to understand their gravity or to deal adequately and realistically with them. Perhaps Brendan communicates more with his actions than with his words; the facts of the case reveal, however, that his messages are generally clear and clearly received. The point here is that, rather than conceptualizing such clients and portraying them to themselves in terms like "can't express anger," "uses humor as a defense mechanism," or "can't communicate," we recognize and appreciate the client's way of doing things so long as we see that "it works."

Conclusion

The policies discussed in this chapter, though assembled in connection with status dynamic psychotherapy, transcend many different treatment modalities and schools of psychotherapy. We regard it as beneficial, for example, to "deal with the reality basis of emotions" or to "go first where you are welcome" regardless of whether one is about to undertake cognitive modification, family restructuring, or status dynamic interventions. For excellent extended treatments of these and further policies, I refer the interested reader to the works of Peter Ossorio (1976) and Richard Driscoll (1984) cited at the end of this book

Chapter 7
Using Images in Psychotherapy

Sarah, a woman in her early thirties, enters psychotherapy. She is deeply concerned about the pattern of her romantic relationships and about her low self-esteem. It seems that she has little problem meeting men and having them pursue her. Further, these men tend to be decent people to whom she finds herself quite attracted. Initially, Sarah is excited and elated with each new relationship. However, if a relationship deepens and the man begins to express affection for her, she finds herself mysteriously losing interest, pulling back, and becoming critical. Soon thereafter, she ends the relationship. Each ending leaves her depressed, wondering why her feelings changed, and despairing that she will ever have a successful love relationship.

Sarah's relationship problem could be addressed in a variety of ways. Her therapist, Peter, however, elects to tell her a story: "When you tell me about this pattern of relationships, Sarah, I am reminded of an old movie scene. Let me share it with you and see if it sheds any light on what's going on here. The story comes from an old W.C. Fields movie in which he plays this seedy old character who lives at the edge of town, down in the bottom land on the wrong side of the tracks. Up on the hill is the local country club, and the country club for him symbolizes everything that he wants. For years, he lives down there, eating his heart out because he doesn't belong. Finally, one golden day, in the mail comes an engraved invitation that says, 'You are hereby invited to be a member of the country club.' He reads the invitation, seems strangely unmoved by it, and turns it down. A good friend of his who knows about all of this has a fit, and after he calms down he demands, 'What the hell are you doing? You've been eating your heart out all these years, and when the invitation comes you turn it down.' To which W.C. Fields makes his famous reply: 'I wouldn't want to be a member of a club that would have anything to do with the likes of me.' Now I'm wondering, Sarah, if this isn't the sort of thing that keeps happening when those men start to care about you, namely..." (adapted from Ossorio, 1976).

This example illustrates one way that status dynamic psychotherapists have traditionally communicated with their clients. Peter, the therapist in this vignette, has elected to introduce a potentially important idea to Sarah by using an *image* – a story, metaphor, or analogy – that he believes may capture the sense of what she is doing with men, that is, disqualifying them precisely on grounds that they accept "the likes of her." Rather than employing more conventional means such as giving literal interpretations or elucidating cognitive schemas, Peter here tells a story that he thinks might shed light both on Sarah's problem and on the direction in which change might take place.

In this chapter, I will (a) relate the many benefits that employing images can have, (b) present guidelines for presenting, clarifying, and applying them to clients' unique situations, and (c) conclude by introducing a number of images with broad clinical utility.

Benefits of Using Images in Psychotherapy

Why images? In my view, images possess a number of inherent virtues that make them particularly effective vehicles for communicating important ideas to clients. These virtues are the subject of this section.

Cognitive Organization

Few clients bring their difficulties to therapy all tied up in a neat intellectual package. Typically, as discussed in chapter 5, they present what is for them a bewildering array of painful feelings, self-characterizations, situations, and life events. Thus, they do not have a solid understanding of what is going on, much less any clear notion of what they can do to resolve their problems.

An image is, among other things, a cognitive package. As exemplified in the W.C. Fields vignette, it usually contains a logical sequence of events that lead to some conclusion. Well tailored to clients' dilemmas, then, an image can, by virtue of this intrinsic property, achieve a number of worthwhile ends. It can help clients observe important relationships that might have escaped them previously – for example, in Sarah's case, the relationship between her self-esteem and her loss of interest in men. Further, an image can highlight certain factors in a client's situation, de-emphasize others, and introduce new ones not previously considered, thus helping clients to distinguish what is relevant and important in their circumstances. A well-tailored image can tie up a previously bewildering array of factors into a more meaningful, understandable, cognitive whole. In doing so, it can help clients achieve a better grasp of their difficulties and discern possible paths to helpful action.

A Resistance Minimizer

An image is on its face a story or illustration about people and situations other than the listener. In weaving such a narrative, the therapist is holding up something "out there," something outside the immediate world of clients, and beckoning them to observe it. Clients are not, at the point of the telling, being called on to look at themselves, but merely to look at the doings of other people, real or fictional, literal or metaphorical.

This externalized mode of presentation has a tendency to result in decreased defensiveness and resistance toward messages contained in the image. While there are a few clients who, during the telling, will be privately self-preoccupied with the question, "What is my therapist saying about *me*?", the great majority become caught up in the image itself. Being so captivated, they are able to listen, to take in, and to ponder its meaning with less defensiveness and resistance than when they must entertain more direct forms of input about themselves.

Staying Power

A good story, particularly one with personal relevance to the listener, has unusually good staying power. Told well and used judiciously, stories stand out from the gestalt of the overall therapeutic conversation, and clients tend to remember them. In my experience, on numerous occasions clients have alluded to stories that I told them months previously in therapy. On one occasion, a friend of mine recalled a story that his therapist had told him eight years previously.

The advantages of this staying power where therapeutic messages are concerned is obviously considerable.

Images and Code Communication

A further advantage of using images in psychotherapy is that they offer a very efficient form of code communication with clients. Once the therapist shares an image, he or she might be able to recapture its entire point or sense merely by using some key word or phrase from the image. Thus the therapist can reintroduce an entire idea, and one perhaps that is complex and time consuming to convey initially, simply by uttering these code words or phrases.

For example, with couples who are prone to conjure up grievances toward each other without checking out their basis in reality, I have often used the old joke about the man who goes next door to borrow a cup of sugar. As he is walking over to his neighbor's house, he starts to think to himself, "I'll bet he's not going to want to lend me any sugar." As he continues on his way, he becomes more and more convinced he will be refused, and more and more angry. Finally, he knocks on the door, and the neighbor answers, but before the neighbor even has a chance to say "hello," the man shouts at him, "Keep your damn sugar!" and stalks off. Once this story has been told, on future occasions when couples relate instances in which they generate anger and grievances in the absence of reality testing, I am able to remind them of what they are doing merely by jokingly chiding them with the words, "Keep your damn sugar." Such private code communication, like many secret meanings shared between people, often serves as a rapport builder between client and therapist.

The Image as Diagnosis

Images are often diagnoses. They are descriptions of what is wrong. They may pertain to what is wrong with the way individuals are *behaving* (as in "keep your damn sugar"), with the way they *are* (as in the example of Sarah and her low self-esteem), or with both (Sarah not only has low self-esteem but also engages in acts of disqualification of the men in her life).

Despite their informal character, good images possess a number of advantages over traditional DSM diagnoses. First, they are clear and non-mystifying to clients. Drawn from the general culture and common fund of knowledge, their content is already familiar to clients, and therefore represents something they can use without having to learn anything new. This clarity and comprehensibility render them superior to DSM diagnoses, which few clients understand.

Second, images permit the clinician to avoid the stigmatizing and other countertherapeutic effects often attendant upon giving clients a DSM diagnosis. In the image's portrayal of a reality in which what is happening to the client is understandable in terms of everyday social relationships and meanings, and is such that paths to change may be discerned, it serves to remove the problem far from the frightening, mystifying, and stigmatizing realms of "mental illness." In contrast, DSM diagnoses are not only, as research has shown, socially stigmatizing, but are viewed by many clients as incomprehensible diseases requiring, like cancer or heart disease, expert (often medical) understanding, and thus represent conditions over which they have little or no personal control.

A third advantage of images over traditional diagnoses is that they are far more precise, that is, far more finely targeted towards exactly what is wrong. Sarah, due to her lack of self-esteem, is concluding that anyone who would accept her must himself be unworthy. Our couple is failing to check out reality before conjuring up grievances toward each other. The images of "W. C. Fields and the country club" and "keep your damn sugar" capture their problems very precisely. In contrast, were we to employ DSM descriptors such as "dysthymic" or "paranoid" or "partner relational problem," these would, even if correct, be far less precise than our images in articulating the nature of the problem.

Fourth and finally, good, well-chosen images are superior to DSM diagnoses in fulfilling the basic objective of a diagnosis: They indicate actions that clients might take to address their problems. Sarah, hearing the W. C. Fields story, realizes that if she can stop reflexively disqualifying men on the highly questionable basis that they care about her, she can make an important change in her relationships. Our couple, on hearing the "keep your damn sugar" image, see its obvious implication that they need to check things out with each other before jumping to negative conclusions. The images contain clear implications, both for clients and therapists, about how change can be brought about, and they are therefore empowering. DSM diagnoses, especially for clients who have been given them, contain few such implications, and are more often than not disempowering.

Some Guidelines for the Use of Images

Customarily, when using images in psychotherapy, the therapist (a) presents the image, (b) elaborates on it if needed to ensure that the client client understands it, and (c) discusses its application to the client's own situation, transforming and paraphrasing it if necessary. Here's an illustration with an image entitled "Balance."

Let us suppose that a couple comes into therapy. They are different from each other in some way. One might be more of a disciplinarian with the children, the other less so. Or one might be more risk-taking, the other more cautious. One might be infused with a philosophy that money is to be spent and life enjoyed; the other is more conservative about money. In any event, in the early stages of their marriage, these differences seemed relatively modest and nonproblematic. Now, however, the couple comes to therapy complaining of extreme differences. The therapist, Sonja, having heard the complaints of each, might simply relate the following image and ask the clients to "try it on for size":

"Think of two parents with a child. Initially, they disagree somewhat about how strict to be with the child. The father thinks the mother is a little too lenient, and the mother thinks the father is a bit too strict, but it's not to the point where it's a big problem. At some point, however, the mother, believing that the father has become a bit more strict than usual, begins to compensate for this by being a little more lenient. When she does that, the father notices and begins to compensate for the

mother's increased leniency by being a little more strict. Then, when he does that, the mother becomes even more lenient to compensate for the father's greater strictness, and the father becomes even more strict to compensate for the mother's increased lenience. And it goes on that way until you find them at polar opposites, where the father is as strict as can be, and the mother is as lenient as can be, and they completely disagree with each other" (adapted from Ossorio, 1976).

Once Sonja shares this image with the couple, she takes care to see that they understand the dynamic exemplified in it. With this particular image, few clients need further elaboration or explication. However, when Sonja is sure the clients understand the image, she discusses its application to their situation. If their issue is the disciplinary one embodied in the story, little application is needed. If it is some other issue, such as spending money or risk taking, Sonja might need to clarify the relevance. Finally, she explores with the couple whether the positive feedback loop described in the image does or does not apply to them. If it does, she can pursue various rather obvious remedies with her clients. One nice feature of the "balance" image is that it clearly illustrates how either partner's unilateral movement back toward a more moderate position would give the other partner reason to make a corresponding adjustment.

At times, this three-step sequence will not have an effect on clients. For example, let us suppose that our couple's problem does lie in the area of the disciplining of children. Sonja presents the "balance" image, but the husband exhibits little interest in modifying his behavior, and insists on the rightness of his extreme stance on discipline. Here, Sonja will likely have to abandon the initial image, which has functioned as a hypothesis, and turn her attention to what it is about this man that results in his intransigence. Is it something characterological? Is it that he would see moderating his behavior as "losing," since he would be giving in to what his wife has been urging all along, and he cannot bear to lose? Depending on what Sonja discovers with this line of exploration, she would turn her attention to addressing it, and might or might not employ further images in doing so.

Images can be used for a variety of purposes. In the present example, the use was straightforward: helping a couple to understand their difficulties and illuminate a path to change. However, in other circumstances, the same image might be used to explain to a client why her parents behaved as they did when she was growing up, and thus to help her judge one or both of them less harshly. Or it might be used to alert a client to the possible negative implications of taking some unilateral action to compensate for a spouse's behavior – for example, might it escalate a situation where they now have only minor disagreement? Images are *devices, not techniques*, and as such can serve a wide variety of purposes. Let's look at a few more examples.

More Images and Their Clinical Applications

"Bowling 300"

This image, suggested to me by Ana Bridges, is directed primarily to clients who are perfectionistic. Upon assessment, I have often found that these individuals employ their standard of perfection in a certain distinct way. Specifically, they employ it as a standard of adequacy in which, if they achieve perfection, they have succeeded, but if they do not achieve perfection, they have failed completely. As a client once expressed the matter, "My standard is perfection, and if I achieve it, which I almost never do, I get a 10. If I fail to achieve it, I get a zero. I don't give any 9.5s like they do in Olympic figure skating."

The image. *"Imagine two bowlers. Both have the same goal: to bowl 300, a perfect game. Bowler number one starts out. He bowls 4 strikes in a row, but in the fifth frame he fails to get a strike. He turns on himself, telling himself that he is a complete failure, that he is inadequate, and that he can never get anything right. Bowler number two starts out. He too bowls 4 strikes in a row, and then fails to get a strike in frame number 5. He is disappointed. He mutters an epithet under his breath. But his internal dialogue is more along the following lines: "Too bad. I had a perfect game going. But I still have a very good game going, and I have a shot at getting over 200, which would be great. And of course, it goes without saying that on my next game I'll be shooting for 300 again, even though I know it's something I might never accomplish in my lifetime."*

Commentary. In this image, both bowlers have a goal to achieve perfection, but they have very different approaches to this goal. For the first bowler, bowling a perfect 300 game is a *standard of adequacy.* Failing to bowl 300 represents total failure and is a cause for turning on himself and questioning his very adequacy. He displays an element of grandiosity here, for the implication of his self-indictment is that he should bowl 300 every time. For the second bowler, the standard of perfection is an ideal or a guidestar. It is a goal that he aims for with unwavering constancy, even while acknowledging that he will only very rarely, and possibly never, achieve it. A clinically useful feature of this image relates to the fact that many perfectionists are not receptive to messages from therapists that say, "You have to relax your standards." For them, this is essentially a call to abandon the pursuit of excellence and to settle for mediocrity, and they are understandably loathe to do this. In contrast, the message of this image is: "You can and should keep your standard of perfection, but you need to use it as a guidestar rather than a standard of adequacy." I have found that this message is far more acceptable, and even welcome, to most perfectionists.

"Poor No More"

This image applies to clients who, despite the fact that they have accomplished things in their lives that they strongly desired, find themselves strangely unhappy. Although they may have achieved the love relationships, family life, friendships, recognition, success, wealth, or other things that they keenly desired, they find themselves curiously unable to derive the kind of joy and satisfaction from these that they expected. The "poor no more" image touches upon one often overlooked reason why people feel this way.

The image: *A child grows up in grinding poverty. It's very painful for him and he hates it. Around the age of 13, it really gets to him and he swears to himself that when he grows up, he's not going to be poor. Twenty years later, he's made his vow come true. He has thirty million* *dollars in the bank, he's making money hand over fist, he's got yachts, cars, houses on the Riviera, and more. But he's not happy.*

The man is puzzled by this. He thinks to himself, 'What's wrong here? It can't be that I haven't reached my goal. I swore I would not be poor when I grew up, and I'm not. I've escaped poverty and put thirty million dollars distance between me and it. It can't be that I don't have the things that money can buy, since I have everything I ever dreamed of and more. Why am I not happier? Why am I not getting the sort of satisfaction out of all this that I think I should be getting?'

One day the answer comes to him. He realizes that his entire life has always been, and continues to be, centered around not being poor, that where he has always been coming from is escaping from that hated, painful condition of his childhood. And, coming from there, the best that he can ever do is to be "poor no more" by avoiding that awful condition. Even if he succeeds entirely, what he succeeds at is avoiding that negative thing, not anything positive. He can never be a success; he can only avoid failure. He can never be rich; he can only be poor no more. If this is the significance he attaches to things, the primary emotions that he can experience can never be the elation or satisfaction that come with a positive achievement; they can only be the relief that comes when he escapes and puts ever-increasing distance between himself and poverty. He is in essence spending his life not being some way and running from that way, and that is a losing game in which the best he can ever do is break even. He can never succeed (adapted from Ossorio, 1976).

Commentary. Some clients spend their lives in a basic mode of escape or avoidance, of not being some way. Often there is something in their past that was terribly painful and intolerable. What they are doing might be escaping poverty, but more often it is something like avoiding being disapproved of, being rejected, being a nobody, being a failure, being unloved, or being a bad parent. When they are successful, the sense they have is not one of joy and celebration, but more one of relief: "Whew, I've avoided disapproval (or failure or rejection or...)." In their minds, they have not achieved a triumph. They have merely escaped that dreaded condition.

"Little White Balls"

The image "little white balls" can be useful for clients who find themselves unable to derive sufficient meaning and satisfaction in their lives. These individuals describe their existence in terms like "empty," "meaningless," and "alienated;" and feel that in their lives or in significant parts thereof, they are "just going through the motions" or "putting in time." While there is more than one reason why persons might be gripped with such a sense, the image addresses one common reason.

The image. Suppose that you walk in and ask me what I've been doing this morning. And I tell you, "Well, I've been walking around on grass and knocking little white balls into holes in the ground, and then doing the whole thing over and over again a total of eighteen times." If I said that, you'd probably say, "Well, why on earth would anyone want to do that? Why would anyone want to walk around all morning knocking little white balls into holes in the ground, and then doing it over and over again?" On the other hand, if I said I'd been playing golf, you wouldn't ask why on earth I'd want to do that, because you know that golf is something that people do appreciate. Not everybody, of course, but many people do play golf and do get something out of it (adapted from Ossorio, 1976).

Commentary. There is little meaning or satisfaction in knocking little white balls into holes in the ground, but there is much meaning and satisfaction for many people in playing golf. Much the same can be said for "pencil pushing" as opposed to "making sure the accounts are in order"; "keeping the rugrats in line until 3:15" as opposed to "educating children"; or "screwing" as opposed to "making love." The overt performance aspects of each of these contrasting pairs may be substantially the same. But what often robs meaning from persons who see their actions in the first of these ways is that they are operating on the level of the concrete behaviors involved, and they are failing to appreciate the broader social practice (or "game") in which they are engaged, and thus the significance of what they are doing.

Consider the following series of descriptions, all equally correct, of a man's actions. Description #1: He is "moving his arm up and down."

Now, we add some contextual information: He is gripping the handle of a water pump as he does so. Thus, description #2: The man is "pumping water." Further context: The pump delivers water to the inhabitants of a house on the hill. Thus, description #3: He is "pumping water to the people in the house on the hill." Further context: The water is poisoned and the man knows it. Thus description #4: He is "poisoning the people in the house on the hill." Yet further context: The people in the house on the hill are plotting to overthrow the duly elected government of their country, and the water pumper knows that, unless he can stop them, their plan stands a good chance of succeeding. Thus description #5: The man is "saving the country." (NB: This analysis is itself an image, one known as "Saving the Nation," and comes originally from the work of Elizabeth Anscombe.)

What is noteworthy in this example is the increased meaningfulness of each new description of what the man is doing. At the lower end, we have "moving his arm up and down," which strikes us as meaningless. At the upper end, after we have learned increasingly *what he is doing by doing that*, we have "saving the nation," a highly meaningful act. Some persons lead their lives, or areas of their lives, focussed on the more concrete, insignificant views of what they are doing. Others recognize and appreciate the higher order significances that might be inherent in their behavior. Where people fix their gaze will be critically important in determining both how they participate in the various spheres of their lives and in the meaning that they derive from them.

"Choosing Your Movements"

This image is addressed primarily to persons who don't feel they know how to have good relationships with others, and who are trying hard to understand what they have to do to succeed. They ask questions like these: "How can I communicate better with my spouse?" "What do I have to do to make friends?" "How can I talk to members of the opposite sex?" or "How do I make conversation at social gatherings?" These individuals have often sought help in the past from the many self-help books and articles that offer specific, concrete advice about such matters, but found that this did not prove sufficiently helpful. These sources, they found, urged them to do such things as "Use 'I' statements," "Make good eye contact," or "Ask him about himself" and while these did not seem bad ideas, neither did they provide adequate answers to their basic questions.

The image. As you sit here, imagine that I ask you what you're going to do when we get through with our conversation. And you tell me that you're going to go out and get in your car and drive home. Then I look at you in surprise, and ask, 'How on earth are you ever going to do that? To even get out of your chair, you've got to put one hand on one arm of the chair, the other on the other arm, and you've got to lean forward in just the right way, and you've got to push at just the right speed, because if you don't push hard enough, you won't make it up, but if you push too hard, you'll fall over on your face. At the same time that you're pushing up with just the proper acceleration, you've got to be extending your feet. Otherwise you fall down. And then, if you succeed at getting up out of the chair, you still have to walk to your car, and that's going to call for...'

If you had to get out of your chair that way – by choosing every discrete movement involved in doing so – you couldn't do it. Fortunately, you don't have to. You get up, walk out, and get in your car by doing what you do know how to do, and that is simply getting up, walking out, and getting in your car. And when you do that, you will have made all the right moves. What you don't have to do is to accomplish this extraordinary feat by choosing all of your movements to be just the right ones (adapted from Ossorio, 1976).

Commentary. This image carries both a negative and a positive message. First the negative: Don't try to solve your relationship problems by attempting to choose highly specific, concrete movements, that is, by determining what precise words to use, sentences to utter, scripts to follow, places to fix one's gaze, and so forth. Approaching it this way, the task becomes impossible. Just as you could never get out of your chair or into your car if you had to do so this way, you cannot solve basic relationship problems this way. While other sorts of human endeavors may respond well to this approach (for example, making a cake or assembling a piece of furniture), it does not work well for accomplishing relationship goals.

Now the positive aspect of the image: Pitch your efforts at the level of bringing about the larger relationship goal you wish to accomplish. While we can't succeed by acting on directions like, "First, accelerate your body with just the right force upward...", we can succeed by acting on goal-centered ones like "stand up." Where human relationships are concerned, we can act on directions like "Figure out what you have to share with this person, and share it," or "Given your current relationship to this person, figure out what you have to say to her, and say it." What you need to worry about in these cases is what you've got to share, or what you've got to say. If you've got something to share or say, the specific words will come.

In marital conflict situations, for example, approaching it in this light would mean that the thrust would become, not "Use I statements," etc., but "Search for a mutually acceptable way to resolve the issue that is dividing us." In blind date situations, the thrust would become, not "Be sure to smile a lot, make eye contact, and ask her about her work," but "Try to get to know her and to let her know me, and see if we click." In such situations, if we resolve the issue that has divided us, or if we get to know each other, our specific words, sentences, smiles, and gazes will have been the right ones.

"The Lion in the Room"

This image, mentioned in chapter 6 in another connection, is used primarily to convey to clients several important points regarding what they need to do to fully and adequately get treatment for their depression, anxiety, or other emotional suffering. It amounts in essence to a way to communicate the policy that they must deal with the reality basis of their emotions, and not just with their feelings. In its quaint way, it also amounts to a simple and utterly clear "position paper" for clients and clinicians on the use and misuse of psychotropic drugs.

The image. Consider the following two very simple scenarios. Scenario #1: A lion walks in the room...you feel scared...you take a happy pill...you don't feel scared anymore...the lion eats you. Scenario #2: A lion walks in the room...you freeze in panic...you take a happy pill...you unfreeze...you run out the back door and escape the lion (adapted from Ossorio, 1976).

Commentary. The first scenario communicates to clients that, if they resort to medications (or other "happy pills" such as meditation or relaxation techniques) as their exclusive response to painful emotional states, they are not addressing the basic source of their problems and are placing themselves in jeopardy. It is critical, therefore, to address the reality basis of these emotions with appropriate and effective action.

The second scenario communicates the point that emotional states such as anxiety, depression, and grief are at times of such proportions that they are immobilizing. They prevent individuals from doing what they need to do to deal with the reality basis of their emotions. In such circumstances, medications are often very helpful in reducing the emotional state and its paralyzing effects. For clients who need medication but are reluctant to take it, this image may make the points that their use of medication (a) would be temporary, (b) would not represent the basic solution to their difficulties, but (c) would instead be a necessary first move that could enable them to solve the basic problem at the root of their emotional pain.

"Starfish"

This image is addressed primarily to persons who find themselves holding a standard for meaningfulness that says, "Unless the doing of something represents a grand and glorious and earthshaking accomplishment, it isn't worth doing." In the face of everyday mundane activities or projects, such people find themselves reluctant to do anything since most things seem so trivial and unimportant.

The image. A man is walking down the beach early one morning. He notices that thousands and thousands of starfish have been washed up on the beach by the tide, and are now stranded and dying. As he walks on, he sees a little girl who is going around picking up starfish, and flinging them with all her might back into the water. He goes up to her just as she is about to fling another and, stopping her, says, 'Little girl, you're wasting your time. Can't you see that there are thousands of starfish here and that it's impossible to get them all back into the ocean. You can't begin to make a difference.' The little girl, after pausing to hear the man out, shrugs and flings the starfish in her hand into the ocean. "I made a difference to that one," she says (adapted from Eiseley, 1979).

Commentary. "It's the measuring stick that kills," a saying has it. If we take as our standard for an action to be worth doing that it must accomplish something on a grand scale, the danger arises that we regard nothing as worth doing, we fail to act, our lives are rendered more meaningless, and the lives of those around us suffer from our paralysis and our grandiosity. If, in contrast, we recognize the value in more modest endeavors, our lives, our ability to act, our sense of meaningfullness, and the lives of others all benefit. The lesson? If one can change the world for the better, by all means change it. But if, like the overwhelming majority of humankind, one cannot, it is critically important to recognize the value in changing one's little corner of the world, and to act on that. In the words of Mother Teresa, "We can do no great things, only small things with great love."

****

Images are powerful devices for assisting clients. When we choose them well and tailor them carefully to our clients' situations, they have many benefits. They reduce clients' confusion by organizing their thinking about their problems. They reduce defensiveness and thus enable clients to better hear important ideas. They tend to be remembered by clients. They provide a very efficient and rapport-building code communication. And, in their homey way, they provide diagnoses of their problems that clients can understand, that are free of stigmatizing implications, and that illuminate paths to change. For a more extensive list of images and their clinical applications, the interested reader is referred to the excellent work of Peter Ossorio (1976) and of Richard Driscoll (1984) on this subject.

Chapter 8
Conclusion

My behavioral colleagues have always argued, "Well, whether you know it or not, and whether you like it or not, you will be reinforcing (or failing to reinforce) your clients, so you better be aware of what you are doing and do it well and carefully." It is the same with status assignments. We *will* assign statuses to our clients. There is no way not to do so. We will regard them as acceptable or unacceptable, powerful or powerless, rational or irrational, resource-possessing or bankrupt, bright or dull, loving or unloving, and so forth. And we will treat them accordingly. Our clients, more often than not, will be strongly affected by our status assigments. They will benefit from them or suffer from them.

Viewed from this vantage point, what I have been urging throughout this book is this: As therapists, be aware of status dynamics – the dynamic articulated in all its many guises throughout this volume – and use it consciously and deliberately to benefit your clients. In the therapeutic relationships you establish, be the assigner of a whole host of pre-determined empowering statuses. In your further interventions, be an active and tireless searcher for others, whether these lie in clients' personal characteristics, relationships to their own problems, positions vis-a-vis important others in their lives, or wherever they may be found. Assign these statuses and treat the client accordingly in everything you do. Take the stance with the client that, "This is who you are and this is who I will treat you as being, unless and until the facts no longer permit me to do so." Carry out this core agenda by employing the status dynamic interventions described throughout this book, and also in the way you implement such proven traditional strategies as cognitive restructuring, behavior rehearsal, exposure therapy, or family restructuring.

For me, these ideas have proven most powerful and effective over the course of more than 30 years of therapy experience. I hope that they will prove of comparable value to you.

References

American Psychiatric Association (1994). *Diagnostic and Statistical Manual of Mental Disorders* (4th ed.). Washington, D.C.: Author.

Anscombe, G.E.M. (1957). *Intention.* Oxford: Blackwell.

Bergner, R. (1979). The use of systems-oriented illustrative stories in marital psychotherapy. *Family Therapy,* 6, 109-118.

Bergner, R. (1981). The overseer regime: A descriptive and practical study of the obsessive compulsive personality style. In K. Davis (Ed.), *Advances in Descriptive Psychology* (Vol. 1, pp. 245-272). Greenwich, CT: JAI Press.

Bergner, R. (1982). Hysterical action, impersonation, and caretaking roles. In K. Davis & T. Mitchell (Eds.), *Advances in Descriptive Psychology* (Vol. 2, pp. 233-248). Greenwich, CT: JAI Press, Inc.

Bergner, R. (1985). Paranoid style: A descriptive and pragmatic account. In K. Davis & T. Mitchell (Eds.), *Advances in Descriptive Psychology* (Vol. 3, pp. 203-230). Greenwich, CT: JAI Press.

Bergner, R. (1987). Undoing degradation. *Psychotherapy,* 24, 25-30.

Bergner, R. (1988). Status dynamic psychotherapy with depressed individuals. *Psychotherapy,* 25, 266-272.

Bergner, R. (1988). Money's 'Lovemap' account of the paraphilias: A critique and reformulation. *American Journal of Psychotherapy,* 42, 254-259.

Bergner, R. (1990). Father-daughter incest: Degradation and recovery from degradation. In A. Putman & K. Davis (Eds.), *Advances in Descriptive Psychology* (Vol. 5, pp. 285-306). Ann Arbor, MI: Descriptive Psychology Press.

Bergner, R. (1990). Impulsive action and impulsive persons: A descriptive and pragmatic formulation. In A. Putman & K. Davis (Eds.), *Advances in Descriptive Psychology* (Volume 5, pp. 261-284). Ann Arbor, MI: Descriptive Psychology Press.

Bergner, R. (1991). Proposal for an eclectic framework. *Journal of Integrative and Eclectic Psychotherapy,* 10, 3, 295-318.

Bergner, R. (1993). Victims into perpetrators. *Psychotherapy,* 30, 452-462.

Bergner, R. (1995). *Pathological Self-Criticism: Assessment and Treatment.* New York: Plenum.

Bergner, R. (1997). What is psychopathology? And so what? *Clinical Psychology: Science and Practice,* 4, 235-248.

Bergner, R. (1998a). Characteristics of an optimal clinical case formulation.

American Journal of Psychotherapy, 52, 287-300.

Bergner, R. (1998b). Therapeutic approaches to problems of meaninglessness. *American Journal of Psychotherapy*, 52, 1-16.

Bergner, R. (1999). Status enhancement: A further path to therapeutic change. *American Journal of Psychotherapy*, 53, 201-214.

Bergner, R. (2002). Sexual compulsion as attempted recovery from degradation. *Journal of Sex and Marital Therapy*, 28, 373-387.

Bergner R. (2003). Emotions: A relational view and its clinical applications. *American Journal of Psychotherapy*, 57, 471-490.

Bergner R (2004). An integrative framework for psychopathology and psychotherapy. *New Ideas in Psychology*, 22, 127-141.

Bergner, R. (2005). Status dynamic treatment of a case of bulimia. *Clinical Case Studies*, 4, 295-303.

Bergner, R., & Staggs, J. (1987). The positive therapeutic relationship as accreditation. *Psychotherapy*, 24, 315-320.

Bergner, R., & Staggs, J. (1991). The positive therapeutic relationship: An accreditation perspective. In M. Roberts & R. Bergner (Eds.), *Clinical Topics: Contributions to the Conceptualization and Treatment of Adolescent Family Problems, Bulimia, Chronic Mental Illness, and Mania* (Vol. 6, pp. 185-202).

Ann Arbor, MI: Descriptive Psychology Press.

Bergner, R. & Holmes, J. (2000). Self-concepts and self-concept change: A status dynamic formulation. *Psychotherapy*, 37, 36-44.

Binswanger, L. (1963). Being-in-the-World. New York: Basic Books.

Camus, A. (1955). The Myth of Sisyphus and Other Essays. New York: Knopf.

Corrigan, P. (2004). How stigma interferes with mental health care. *American Psychologist*, 59, 614-625.

Driscoll, R. (1984). *Pragmatic Psychotherapy*. New York: Van Nostrand Reinhold.

Eisely, L. (1979). *The Star Thrower*. New York: Harcourt.

Farber, A. (1981). Castaneda's Don Juan as psychotherapist. In K. Davis (Ed.), *Advances in Descriptive Psychology* (Vol. 1, pp. 279-304). Greenwich, CT: JAI Press.

Frankl, V. (1969). *The Will to Meaning*. New York: World.

Garfinkel, H. (1957). Conditions of successful degradation ceremonies.*American Journal of Sociology*, 63, 420-424.

Goffman, E. (1963). *Stigma: Notes on the Management of Spoiled Identity*. Englewood Cliffs, NJ: Prentice-Hall.

Horney, K. (1945). *Our Inner Conflicts*. New York: Norton.

Jeffrey, J. (1998). Cognition without processes. In J. Jeffrey & R. Bergner

(Eds.), *Advances in Descriptive Psychology* (Vol. 7, pp. 33-66). Ann Arbor, MI: Descriptive Psychology Press.

Keane, T., & Barlow, D. (2002). Post-Trauamatic Stress Disorder. In D. Barlow (Ed.), *Anxiety and its Disorders: The Nature and Treatment of Anxiety and Panic* (2d ed.). New York: Guilford.

Kernberg, O. (1975). *Borderline Conditions and Pathological Narcissism*. New York: Jason Aronson.

Kihlstrom, J., & Klein, S. (1994). The self as a knowledge structure. In R. Wyer & T. Srull (Eds.), *Handbook of Social Cognition* (2d ed., pp. 152-208). Hillsdale, NJ: Erlbaum.

Kirsch, N. (1982). Attempted suicide and restrictions in the ability to negotiate personal characteristics. In K. Davis & T. Mitchell (Eds.), *Advances in Descriptive Psychology* (Vol. 2, pp. 249-274). Greenwich, CT: JAI Press.

Koestner, R., Zuroff, D., & Powers, T. (1991). Family origins of adolescent self-criticism and its continuity into adulthood. *Journal of Abnormal Psychology*, 100, 191-197.

Lewin, K. (1936). *Principles of Topological Psychology*. New York: McGraw

Link, B., & Phelan, J. (2001). Conceptualizing stigma. *Annual review of sociology*, 27, 363-385.

Marshall, K. (1985). Scenarios of 'alcoholic' relationships. In K. Davis & T. Mitchell (Eds.), *Advances in Descriptive Psychology* (Vol. 3., pp. 259-280). Greenwich, CT: JAI Press.

Marshall, K. (1993). A bulimic life pattern. In R. Bergner (Ed.), *Studies in Psychopathology: The Descriptive Psychology Approach*. Ann Arbor, MI: Descriptive Psychology Press. (Original work published, 1985)

McNally, R. (1999). EMDR and mesmerism. *Journal of Anxiety Disorders*, 13, 225-36.

Messer, S., & Wampold, B. (2002). Let's face it: Common factors are more potent than specific therapy ingredients. *Clinical Psychology: Science and Practice*, 9, 21-25.

Miller, W., & Rollnick, S. (2002). *Motivational Interviewing* (2d. ed.). New York: Guilford.

Minuchin, S. (1974). *Families and Family Therapy*. Cambridge, MA: Harvard University Press.

O'Hanlon, W., & Weiner-Davis, M. (2003). *In Search of Solutions* (2d. ed.). New York: Norton.

Ossorio, P. G. (1976). *Clinical Topics: A Seminar in Descriptive Psychology*. Whittier, CA and Boulder, CO: Linguistic Research Institute.

Ossorio, P.G. (1981). An outline of Descriptive Psychology for personality theory and clinical application. In K. Davis (Ed.), *Advances in Descriptive Psychology,* Vol. 1 (pp. 57-82). Greenwich, CT: JAI Press.

Ossorio, P.G. (1985). An overview of Descriptive Psychology. In K. Gergen & K. Davis (Eds.), *Social Construction of the Person.* New York: Springer-Verlag.

Ossorio, P. G. (1990). Appraisal. In A. Putman & K. Davis (Eds.), *Advances in Descriptive Psychology* (Vol. 5, pp. 155-172). Ann Arbor, MI: Descriptive Psychology Press.

Ossorio, P. G. (1995). *Persons.* Ann Arbor, MI: Descriptive Psychology Press. (Original work published, 1966)

Ossorio, P.G. (1997). *Essays on Clinical Topics.* Ann Arbor, MI: Descriptive Psychology Press.

Ossorio, P. G. (1997). Pathology. In P. Ossorio (Ed.), *Essays on Clinical Topics* (pp. 1-70). Ann Arbor, MI: Descriptive Psychology Press. (Original work published, 1985).

Ossorio, P.G. (1998). *Place.* Ann Arbor, MI: Descriptive Psychology Press. (Original work published, 1982)

Ossorio, P. G. (2005). *"What Actually Happens": The Representation of Real World Phenomena.* Ann Arbor, MI: Descriptive Psychology Press. (Original work published, 1978).

Ossorio, P. G. (2006). *The Behavior of Persons.* Ann Arbor, MI: Descriptive Psychology Press. (Original work published, 1977).

Persons, J. (1989). *Cognitive Therapy in Practice.* New York: Norton.

Peterson, C., Maier, S., & Seligman, M. (1993). Learned Helplessness: *A Theory for the Age of Personal Control.* New York: Oxford University Press.

Putman, A. (1981). Communities. In K. Davis (Ed.), *Advances in Descriptive Psychology,* (Vol. 1, pp. 195-210). Greenwich, CT: JAI Press.

Putman, A. (1990). Organizations. In A. Putman & K. Davis (Eds.), *Advances in Descriptive Psychology,* (Vol.5, pp. 11-46). Ann Arbor, MI: Descriptive Psychology Press.

Putman, A. (1998). Being, becoming, and belonging. In In J. Jeffrey & R. Bergner (Eds.), *Advances in Descriptive Psychology* (Vol. 7, pp. 127-162). Ann Arbor, MI: Descriptive Psychology Press.

Raimy, V. (1975). *Misconceptions of the Self.* San Francisco: Jossey-Bass.

Raskin, N., & Rogers, C. (2005). Person-centered therapy. In R. Corsini & D. Wedding (Eds.), *Current Psychotherapies* (7th ed., pp. 130-165). Belmont, CA: Brooks-Cole.

Roberts, M. (1985). Worlds and world reconstruction. In K. Davis &

T. Mitchell (Eds.). *Advances in Descriptive Psychology* (Vol. 4, pp. 17-54). Greenwich, CT: JAI Press.

Roberts, M. (1985). I and thou: A study of personal relationships. In K. Davis & T. Mitchell (Eds.), *Advances in Descriptive Psychology* (Volume 4, pp. 231-258). Greenwich, CT: JAI Press.

Roberts, M. (1991). Psychotherapy with adolescents and their families: A status dynamic approach. In M. Roberts & R. Bergner (Eds.), *Clinical Topics: Contributions to the Conceptualization and Treatment of Adolescent Family Problems, Bulimia, Chronic Mental Illness, and Mania* (Vol. 6, pp. 235-256). Ann Arbor, MI: Descriptive Psychology Press.

Rogers, C. (1951). *Client Centered Therapy*. Boston: Houghton-Mifflin.

Rogers, C. (1957). The necessary and sufficient conditions of therapeutic personality change. *Journal of Consulting Psychology*, 21, 95-103.

Schact, J., Binder, J., & Strupp, H. (1984). The dynamic focus. In H. Strupp & J. Binder (Eds.), *Psychotherapy in a New Key*. New York: Basic Books.

Schwartz, W. (1979). Degradation, accreditation, and rites of passage. *Psychiatry*, 42, 138-146.

Schulz, C. (1968). *Peanuts*. Boulder, CO: The Boulder Daily Camera, May 17, 1968.

Seligman, M. (1975). *Helplessness: On Depression, Development, and Death*. San Francisco: Freeman.

Shapiro, F. (2001). *Eye Movement Desensitization and Reprocessing: Basic Principles and Procedures* (2d. ed). New York: Guilford.

Swann, W. (1992). Seeking "truth," finding despair: Some unhappy consequences of a negative self-concept. *Current Directions in Psychological Science*, 1, 15-18.

Sweet, A. (1984). The therapeutic relationship in behavior therapy. *Clinical Psychology Review*, 4, 253-272.

Watzlawick, P., Weakland, J., & Fisch, R. (1974). *Change: Principles of Problem Formation and Problem Resolution*. New York: Norton.

Wechsler, R. (1991). Personality and manic states: A status dynamic formulation of bipolar disorder. In M. Roberts & R. Bergner (Eds.), *Clinical Topics: Contributions to the Conceptualization and Treatment of Adolescent Family Problems, Bulimia, Chronic Mental Illness, and Mania* (Vol. 6, pp. 203-234). Ann Arbor, MI: Descriptive Psychology Press.

Wilson, G. (2005). Behavior therapy. In R. Corsini & D. Wedding (Eds.), *Current Psychotherapies* (7th ed., pp. 202-237). Belmont,

CA: Brooks-Cole.
Wittgenstein, L. (1953). *Philosophical Investigations*. New York:
Macmillan.
Worden, W. (2002). *Grief Counseling and Grief Therapy* (3d ed.).
New York: Springer.
Yalom, I. (1980). *Existential Psychotherapy*. New York: Basic.

Index

A
Aaron Beck 7
accreditation 12, 18, 19, 26, 27, 28, 31, 67
accreditation ceremony 12
accrediting status 31, 65, 67
accrediting statuses 12
accrediting status assignments 31
actors xi, 57
agent 18, 31
agents of change xi
Albert Ellis 7
alcoholic relationships 5
ally and collaborator 20, 31
ambivalence 64, 93, 94
analogies 8
Ana Bridges ix, 106
anxiety 38, 45, 71, 72, 73, 76, 78, 86, 87, 112, 113
appraisal 16, 28, 53, 55, 56, 66, 86
assertive behaviors 6
assessment 7, 41, 61, 69, 70, 73, 76, 80, 81, 94, 96, 106
assignment 3, 15, 16, 18, 20, 27, 57, 62, 64, 67
author 2, 49
Axis I DSM 5
a priori 11, 12, 13, 14, 15, 16, 17, 20, 22, 82

B
behavioral possibilities 37, 55, 60
behavior potential 4, 5, 14, 26, 39, 61, 62, 65
behavior rehearsal 6, 61, 115
benefit of the doubt 19, 31
Bowling 300 106
Boys' Town 11, 15
Buckminster Fuller 87, 88
bulimia 5, 90

C
Carl Rogers 6, 15, 16, 25
Catcher in the Rye 66
central underlying mechanism 82
Charles Darwin 33
Charles Schulz 14
Charlie Brown 14, 16, 19, 33, 35, 37, 38, 39, 54, 55
chess 35, 54, 55
choice principles 8
Choosing Your Movements 110
clinical assessment 69, 80
clinical case formulation 7, 81
cognitive restructuring 6, 61, 115
common factors 8, 85
consciousness 3, 27, 38, 39, 94
con man 62, 63, 64, 65
credible status assigner 12
critic 4, 15, 25, 29
cultural standards 25
culture 23, 25, 31, 56, 103

D
degrading status assignments 15
depression 5, 26, 61, 67, 70, 72, 86, 87, 112, 113
detective model 76, 94
diagnoses 8, 102, 103, 104, 114
Don't buy victim acts 91
DSM-IV 80, 81
dynamic focus 82

E
Ebenezer Scrooge 62, 64
Edward Albee 25
Eleanor Roosevelt 59
eligibilities 4, 11, 12, 16, 34, 35, 38
Elizabeth Anscombe 110
EMDR 45, 46
empowering statuses xi, 115

personal attribute labels 14
personal change xi
persons xi, xii, 7, 14, 16, 18, 19, 20, 23, 24, 31, 34, 35, 36, 38, 39, 48, 54, 55, 56, 59, 60, 61, 89, 92, 109, 110, 113
place 3, 14, 15, 19, 23, 34, 35, 37, 38, 39, 40, 41, 52, 54, 56, 58, 61, 64, 65, 66, 74, 78, 80, 100
placeholder 29
places xi, xii, 14, 82, 111
places of power xi, xii
policies 8, 85, 86, 97
poopie contest 88
Poor No More 107
position xi, 2, 3, 4, 5, 11, 12, 14, 15, 20, 21, 25, 29, 30, 37, 38, 39, 40, 49, 52, 53, 54, 55, 56, 57, 58, 59, 60, 61, 62, 72, 81, 83, 86, 89, 92, 95, 96, 105, 112
positive therapeutic relationship 6, 11, 12, 16, 19, 20, 30, 31
power xi, xii, 2, 4, 5, 6, 7, 8, 19, 20, 23, 43, 46, 52, 59, 74, 81, 83, 89, 90, 95, 96, 101, 102
presenting concern 4, 76, 78, 88, 94
problems in living 5
problems of adolescence 5
psychotherapists 1, 7, 15, 49, 78, 93, 96, 100
psychotherapy 1, 4, 5, 6, 7, 8, 20, 30, 40, 45, 60, 85, 90, 97, 99, 102, 104
psychotic 17
PTSD 43, 44

R
reality basis of emotions 86, 97
reality constraints 37
reconstructed worlds xi
relational position 2, 3, 14
resistance to change xi, 7, 57, 60
responsible authorship 3

S
Salvador Minuchin 82
Saving the Nation 110